The EMOTIONS
Facts, Theories, and a New Model

STUDIES IN PSYCHOLOGY

Consulting Editors:

L. JOSEPH STONE
AND DWIGHT W. CHAPMAN

Vassar College

The
EMOTIONS
Facts, Theories, and a New Model

⊂⊅ ⊂⊅

by Robert Plutchik
HOFSTRA UNIVERSITY

RANDOM HOUSE
NEW YORK

To the Memory of
My Mother and Brother

<hr />

Foreword

There has long existed the need for a presentation of the leading theories of emotion in more detail than is ordinarily provided by introductory texts and more briefly than provided by specialized volumes. Dr. Plutchik carries out this task in the important context of a theory coming from activities at the grass-roots—out of actual problems growing from experiments on emotion in which he was participating. These experiments raised difficulties concerning measurement and also the need to separate out the components of the complex emotions aroused. Much of the strength of the theory lies in its attempt to deal with these central problems.

In the process of developing his theory, the author presents in some detail a model of primary emotions and their mixtures which has certain affinities in these respects to the theories of James and Wundt. To this he adds the notion of *prototype* behavior patterns which are to be found throughout the phylogenetic scale—a notion which provides an evolutionary rationale for this concept.

The author's clear and succinct statement of the issues which have long plagued writers on emotion should go a long way in helping to clarify the area. He considers the problem of intensity—the variation in amount of emotion; the problem of persistence—the lastingness of the emotion in the contrasting typical laboratory and chronic disease states; the problem of purity—the simple laboratory emotional responses as opposed to the complex clinical expressions of emotion; the problem of individual differences —the naïve assumption that given equivalent stimulus situations the responses may be assumed to be variants around a generalized mean; the problem of introspection

—the complexity of the problem of the "feelings" attached to emotions; and finally, the problem of definition.

Of particular value is his broad approach to the consideration of emotion as seen in the laboratory and as found in the clinic. A major disadvantage of most earlier works in this field has been the sharp dichotomy between the presentation of concrete material from these two sources. Either the laboratory material has been given superficially or the clinical material presented in that remote manner which betrays a lack of first-hand knowledge. In this volume there is clear indication of first-hand knowledge of the phenomena in both fields. The same advantage holds for the breadth of the points of view represented. The catholic use of material deriving from various theoretical viewpoints, for instance from both the psychoanalytic and the behavioristic, makes for a comprehensive approach.

A further contribution of the volume lies in the section devoted to the use of the theory to determine its "direct empirical significance." The experiments given as examples are necessarily inadequate to cover the range of a theory of the breadth of the present one. However, these chapters together with some of the implications of the final chapter which deals in part with psychotherapy and delinquency offer adequate sample tests of the value of the theory in the empirical setting.

All in all the present volume offers an excellent second step toward deeper knowledge of that still relatively neglected area: *the emotions.*

DAVID SHAKOW

National Institute of Mental Health
Bethesda, Md.

Preface

In the summer of 1953, I had the opportunity to participate in a research project concerned with the recording of physiological changes in mental patients during psychiatric interviews. The patients were cooperative and the equipment excellent, yet conclusions were difficult to come by.

As I thought about this, it seemed to me that the major difficulty was our inability to evaluate the patients' emotions. Of particular importance was the fact that their emotions were always mixed, and difficult to specify or unravel.

This observation suggested a possible parallel between mixed emotions and mixed colors. We notice, for instance, that certain hues such as red and green or yellow and blue are complementary or opposite. This is also true of emotions: joy and sorrow, love and hate, acceptance and rejection. How far do the parallels hold? Chapters 4 and 8 suggest, I believe, the surprising number of similarities that actually do exist. Later, as I reviewed the literature, I discovered that several other psychologists, among them William James and Wilhelm Wundt, had suggested a similar analogy.

As I began to develop the implications of such a concept, I gradually discovered other questions that required answering. For example, if we can describe emotions in human adults and in infants and can refer to emotions in primates, dogs, cats, and rats, then at what phylogenetic level can we draw a line and conclude that emotions no longer exist? Consideration of this and other questions gradually led me to the idea of *prototype patterns*, which are basic behavioral reactions identifiable at all evolutionary levels. These patterns change and are modified by evolution, by growth, and by learning.

I began to recognize, too, that an intimate relationship exists between emotions and personality and that the latter in some sense represents emotions which have become mixed and "frozen" in the course of an individual's lifetime. Thus what began as an attempt to explore an analogy had far-reaching implications and suggested experiments, some of which were performed and are reported in this book. Many other research possibilities exist and these are noted at appropriate points.

It should be noted that the analogy is not inviolable; like any model, it is useful primarily as a guide to thinking about problems and is subject to modification in the light of new data and experience. Hopefully the theory even in its present form provides some useful insights, integrations, and research ideas for both the clinically-oriented psychologist and the laboratory experimentalist.

There is no doubt that there have been many influences on my thinking other than those already noted. Of special significance were the comments made by students and colleagues when these ideas were presented as formal addresses at Bard, Hofstra, and Oberlin Colleges, The Nebraska Psychiatric Institute, The University of Cincinnati, Yeshiva University, The Hebrew University of Jerusalem, and the National Institute of Mental Health.

Very useful suggestions concerning the manuscript were made by Dr. Dwight Chapman, Dr. L. Joseph Stone, Dr. Mortimer Mishkin, Dr. Bryan Robinson, and Dr. Gordon Allen. Others who read parts of the manuscript or earlier versions and made thoughtful comments included Dr. David Shakow, Dr. Morris Parloff, and Dr. Harold Henderson. My thanks to Dr. Henry Kellerman for the careful preparation of the index.

I wish also to extend my appreciation to Dr. Richard Trumbull, Director of the Psychological Sciences Division of the Office of Naval Research who provided me, through an ONR contract, both encouragement and funds for the preparation of the manuscript.

R. P.

Contents

Tables and Figures

The EMOTIONS

Facts, Theories, and a New Model

1 ⊂⊐

What Is a Theory of Emotion?

Superstition, prejudice, dogmas form a human record vast and dismal, a permanent warning of the dangers attending the life of reason. From moods to philosophies the affects rule.

—JOSEPH JASTROW

The Problem

The emotions have always been of central concern to men. In every endeavor, in every major human enterprise, the emotions are somehow involved. Almost every great philosopher from Aristotle to Spinoza, from Kant to Dewey, from Bergson to Russell has been concerned with the nature of emotion and has speculated and theorized about its origins, expressions, effects, its place in the economy of human life. Theologians have recognized the significance of certain emotions in connection with religious experience and have made the training of emotions a central, if implicit, part of religious training. Writers, artists, and musicians have always attempted to appeal to the emotions, to affect and move the audience through symbolic communication. And the development in the last half century of psychoanalysis, clinical psychology, and psychosomatic medicine has brought the role of emotion in health and disease sharply to our attention.

Academic psychology too, has recognized the importance of understanding emotion within the framework of its evolving concepts, and every textbook in the field delegates a chapter or two to a discussion of this topic. The development of comparative psychology and behaviorism has contributed considerable impetus to the observation of emotional behavior in animals. There have been literally thousands of papers and reports written dealing with this question. *Yet today there is no single, integrating, comprehensive theory of the emotions which has relevance to all these areas of concern.*

In 1927, Young wrote, "The confusion and contradiction found today within affective psychology are notorious. Upon the most fundamental matters there is little agreement among psychologists." The following year, at the Wittenberg Symposium on "Feelings and Emotion," Claparède echoed the same sentiment. "The psychology of affective processes is the most confused chapter in all psychology."

One would think that after a quarter of a century there might be some change in this situation, some conceptual clarifications concerning the nature and role of emotions. One of the characteristics of science, after all, is the gradual and progressive increase in knowledge which is then reflected in increased understanding, control, and prediction. Yet Hebb in 1949 wrote, "The discussion of emotion has been about as confused as that of any topic in psychology, partly because the terminology is often equivocal and partly because tradition carries great weight in this part of the field."

Two other explanations have been offered for this general state of affairs. Rapaport (1950) suggests that "The main difficulty in the literature of emotions appears to be that the word *emotion* is sometimes used to designate a *phenomenon,* and sometimes to designate the *dynamics* underlying a phenomenon or group of phenomena." Approaching it from a somewhat different point of view, Leeper (1948) writes that "in our thinking about emotion . . . we have been dominated by *a priori* conceptions. Too commonly we have adopted, for all practical purposes, a faulty representation of psychological functions which was started back in the late 1700's—a division of psychological processes into those of cognition, affection, and conation."

The problem of developing a satisfactory psychology of emotion is still with us. Whether the reasons for this are related to the burden of tradition, or confused terminology, or a priori conceptions, or a variety of other problems (as we shall see), it is evident that there is need for an integrated theory of the emotions.

What Is a Theory of Emotion?

In order to accomplish any given end, it is necessary to have some clear notion of what the goal is, and this requires in the present context a statement of what is meant by the word "theory." Such an elaboration may even help provide some of the reasons for the inadequacies of previous analyses. What should a theory of emotion do for us?

First and foremost, a theory should provide answers to a whole series of questions which psychologists have been asking for a long time, such questions as the following. What is an emotion? What produces emotion? What functions do emotions have? Is emotion the cause of a bodily state, the bodily state itself, or the result of a bodily state? What are the physiological changes that are associated with emotion? What are the expressive or overt changes in emotion? What subjective changes are associated with emotions? Can there be emotions without awareness? What is the relation between feelings and bodily states in emotion? How does a person gain "control" over his emotions? To what extent do maturation and learning affect emotion? What relations exist between maladjustment and emotions? How many emotions are there? Are emotions learned or innate? Is there any consistent genetic course of development of emotions? Are emotions disruptive or organizing? Are there differences between emotions? What is the relation between emotion and motivation? How are emotions related to personality?

These are the kinds of questions that are most often asked about emotions, and any adequate theory should either provide an answer (even if tentative) to each of these questions, or indicate the kind of evidence that must be sought in order to answer them.

Theory as Integrator, Predictor, Stimulator, and Incorporator

THEORY AS INTEGRATOR

Not only should a theory of emotion answer in some sense the various questions that have been posed, but it should act to integrate and explain the many things we already accept as fact. This function of theory as *an integrator of facts already known* should not be minimized. Theories always start with known facts, and attempt to integrate them within a single framework and account for them in terms of a small number of basic concepts. Sometimes a theory may indicate that previously accepted statements have to be interpreted in a new way. For example, Einstein held that "the formulation of a problem is often more essential than its solution, which may be merely a matter of mathematical or experimental skill. To raise new questions, new possibilities, to regard old problems from a new angle, requires creative imagination and marks real advance in science."

THEORY AS PREDICTOR

This function of theory as an integrator takes precedence over another of the functions sometimes ascribed to it, *the prediction of new relationships*. It is very likely that this function of theory has been overstated and overrated. Theories rarely predict entirely new relations or new facts in any field of science; if they did, there would be no need for experimentation. *New facts and relationships come primarily from new experiments and new observations.* Einstein's theory of relativity, when first formulated, predicted only one or two entirely unexpected facts (which were later verified); its value lay primarily in showing that many already known observations and some apparent contradictions could be accounted for and resolved in terms of a relatively small number of concepts. It also acted as an integrator of new data as they were collected. In a similar sense, the prediction of new relationships by a theory of emotion might be considered as an "extra dividend" if it also serves to integrate in some consistent way data already known.

THEORY AS STIMULATOR OF RESEARCH

A third and related function of theory is *as stimulator of research.* Any adequate theory will indicate gaps in our knowledge that require filling and provide a spur to certain kinds of studies. The James-Lange theory, for example, stimulated considerable research on autonomic activity in human beings and in animals; psychoanalysis stimulated research dealing with infants, with child development, and with personality. Any new theory of emotion must have implications for research.

THEORY AS INCORPORATOR

A fourth function of theory sometimes overlooked is to *show relationships between apparently diverse areas.* Hecht's photochemical theory, for example, related brightness discrimination, as well as other visual functions, to the biochemistry of the retina; the Gestalt psychologists try to relate complex perceptions to hypothetical brain states. Regardless of the adequacy of any particular attempt, when successful it brings together two realms of phenomena and increases the generality of our concepts. It then means that knowledge obtained independently in one discipline (e.g., the biochemistry of the retina) can be used to predict observations in another (e.g., visual threshold behavior). In general, it is desirable to have a theory which ties together or incorporates apparently unrelated data. Incorporation may be thought of as somewhat different from integration in that it relates different areas of investigation rather than different facts within an area.

The Use of Constructs

In addition to those functions already mentioned, theories also use certain kinds of procedures or methods of approach; these might be described as *constructs, analysis* and *synthesis,* and *analogy.*

Theories in general try to explain or account for a large number of observations in terms of a small number of basic interrelated concepts. These basic concepts usually refer to states, conditions, or events whose properties are known only indirectly through a series of inferences. In psychoanalytic theory, concepts like libido, fixation, repression, or superego refer to hypothetical states or conditions whose properties are gradually derived on the basis of increasing evidence. In contemporary learning theory, such notions as reaction potential, neural oscillation, cognitive maps, or cell assemblies are also hypothetical constructs whose properties are inferred. This idea is more general than might at first appear. Even such apparently simple concepts as pure water, pure hydrogen, pure white, or pure black are actually hypothetical limiting states whose properties are known only as the limit of an infinite progression. There are always impurities or mixtures in every physically real state which modify to some degree the state being observed. This means that our knowledge of these constructs develops gradually only by a series of successive approximations.

One other important aspect of theory construction is that the basic terms or constructs of a theory do not necessarily have to accord with common sense, so long as the experiences of common sense can ultimately be derived from them. To most scholars of the Middle Ages, Galileo's principle of inertia, that bodies will move in a straight line with constant speed, unless an agent or force is applied, seemed incomprehensible. The development of quantum physics at the turn of the century involved assumptions contrary to both common sense and well-established laws of mechanics. Yet the ultimate justification was the new-found ability to predict observed phenomena and to relate diverse observations.

Analysis and Synthesis

There is in most theories an attempt to conceive of a complex phenomenon as the result of the interaction of a variety of simple causes or units. In chemistry, the millions of naturally occurring substances are shown to result from the mixture of a relatively few kinds of elements, and these in turn result from the interaction of an even smaller number of units of matter. This process of reducing a compound or mixture to its elements is called *analysis*.

Freud (1935) has written that in psychiatry "Our path has been like that of chemistry; the great qualitative differences between substances were traced back to quantitative variations in the proportions in which the same elements were combined." This idea of analyzing complex mixtures into simpler units is at the core of attempts by psychologists to find basic personality dimensions and basic personality types. The same path has been taken in trying to understand the phenomena of color mixture; the manifold colors of daily experience can be analyzed into combinations of a few basic primaries or pure colors.

This process of analysis, however, is only part of the process of achieving understanding. If the analysis is an adequate one, then it should be possible to recombine the units in suitable proportions and thereby reconstruct the original complex mixture. This process of *synthesis* is illustrated by the mixture of three primary colors to match any other given colors, or by the combination by chemists of carbon, hydrogen, oxygen, and a few other elements to produce almost any organic substance. The same should be true of any psychological theory as well.

Analogy

In understanding any relatively unexplored area or one in which much disagreement prevails, it is often useful to precede by analogy. Thus we use the known as a model to guide our thinking about the unknown. Physicist Robert Oppenheimer has elaborated on this idea in the following way (1956):

> Whether or not we talk of discovery or of invention, analogy is inevitable in human thought, because we come to new things in science with what equipment we have, which is how we have learned to think, and above all how we have learned to think about the relatedness of things. We cannot, coming into something new, deal with it except on the basis of the familiar and the old-fashioned. . . . This is not to say that analogy is the criterion of truth . . . But truth is not the whole thing; certitude is not the whole of science. Science is an immensely creative and enriching experience; and it is full of novelty and exploration; and it is in order to get to these that analogy is an indispensable instrument. Even analysis, even the ability to plan experiments, even the ability to sort things out and pick them apart presupposes a good deal of structure, and that structure is characteristically an analogical one.

An excellent illustration of the extent of analogical thinking in science may be given by reference to the contemporary development of the analogue computer. Its basic operation relates to the fact that a mathematic expression which describes the behavior of one system also describes the behavior of all other analogous systems. The computer is programed to behave as an analogous system, so that extreme conditions not easily obtained in the natural environment may be studied, and so that the complex interrelations of variables may be analyzed. Analogue computers have been used in nuclear physics, meteorology, medical research, and economic forecasting, thus suggesting the parallel nature of operation of systems in various branches of science. In physics, force in a linear system is analogous to pressure in a fluid system and voltage in an electrical system. Many other analogies are found including the mathematical equations used to describe the relations between such quantities.

Similarly reasoning by analogy was an important part of the development of the theory of evolution; and in chemistry, before the periodic table was developed, a very similar scheme called the law of octaves was proposed, based on analogy with musical scales. All mathematical models used in any science are forms of analogy.

Types of Theory

There has been considerable discussion in psychology on the method of developing the basic theoretical terms of any theory. Some writers have argued that they should simply be summarizing terms for a group of observations (intervening variables), while others have argued that the theoretical terms should refer to events, processes, or entities not directly observed but only inferred (hypothetical constructs).

This kind of distinction has apparently concerned scientists for a long time and many scientists and philosophers have proposed similar dichotomies. Thus in the last century, distinctions were made between abstractive theories and hypothetical theories, between descriptive and explanatory science, and between a principle of causality and a principle of legality, distinctions which relate closely to those made in psychology.

Both approaches have been used in the history of science and are really supplementary rather than opposed. Some of the unobserved entities of physics, like the ether, have proven unfruitful and been given up, while others, like the electron, have had their properties measured in a large variety of independent ways. In fact, the essential criterion of the adequacy of an hypothetical construct is whether its assumed properties can be measured and checked in several different ways (Plutchik, 1954).

It may be said, in summary, that there is no a priori way of deciding in advance which kind of theoretical approach will be most fruitful and that only continuing research and analysis will justify or refute the types of theoretical concepts and relationships used.

The theory of emotion to be presented in this book will utilize all of the procedures described. It will attempt both an analysis and a synthesis of the complex emotions of everyday life; it will conceive of the units of analysis as ideal states or hypothetical constructs, and it will use an analogy to guide its development. Hopefully the theory will be judged in terms of its usefulness in integrating known observations within a consistent framework, suggesting new ones, and relating apparently diverse ideas.

2

Problems for a Theory of Emotion

*No relationship can be defined without a logical
frame and any apparent disharmony in the description of experiences can be eliminated only by
an appropriate widening of the conceptual framework. This lesson . . . has been enforced by the
development of physics in a way that has a bear-
ing on many other fields of human knowledge and
interest in which we meet with similar situations
in the analysis and synthesis of experience.*

—NIELS BOHR

There are a variety of reasons for the confusion
about the nature of emotion. For one thing, the material
and approach of the experimental psychologist differs from
that of the clinician. For another, there are inadequacies
in the experimental approach itself. Finally the analysis of
what a definition of emotion requires is often faulty. This
chapter will attempt an analysis and clarification of these
various problems.

Intensity

Our daily language and experience recognize that emotions may exist in varying degrees of intensity. We often

distinguish between apprehension, anxiety, fear, and panic or between contentment, pleasure, happiness, joy, and ecstasy. Yet strangely enough, psychologists have rarely examined this dimension of variation of emotion. The typical experiment that is reported simply notes the presence or absence of a particular emotion, such as anxiety, tension, fear, or resentment without specifying the relative intensity despite the fact that two different studies designed to produce fear, for example, may produce it to such different degrees that overt or physiological measures obtained may be quite different.

It has been known for a long time that many drugs or chemicals in small quantities have certain pleasant, beneficial effects on the body but are harmful or deadly in large quantities. Small amounts of strychnine increase appetite and muscle activity, while large amounts produce rigidity and death. In 1922, Krogh reported that in carnivorous mammals, infinitesimal doses of histamine, adrenalin, or acetylcholine injected into the blood stream produce a fall of arterial blood pressure. In larger doses, acetylcholine has a pure "depressor" action, which can be ascribed to dilation of arteries; adrenalin shows the well-known "pressor" effect, due to contraction of the arteries, and histamine induces the characteristic symptoms of shock in animals that are susceptible to its action. Since these are some of the drugs related to the appearance of emotional symptoms, it would appear that a more intense arousal of an emotion might introduce different patterns of reactivity.

In his study of fear and anger, Ax (1953) was aware of this problem and tried to equate the intensity of the two emotions produced in the laboratory. Were it not for this, the qualitative differences between fear and anger could have been attributed to a difference in the intensity of arousal of the response rather than to the emotion per se. This fact, the possibility of producing an emotion of varying intensity, may account for some of the differences in the results of different investigators, even those using the same laboratory procedures. Therefore it is necessary to study the physical, the physiological, and the subjective concomitants of emotional states as a function of the intensity of the emotion. Moreover adequate scaling procedures must be developed so that the magnitude or intensity of the emotional state can be unequivocally specified.

In recent years, there has been some concern with the "level of activation" as a psychological concept. This corresponds to the idea of intensity of emotion on a continuum from deep sleep to great excitement, as in rage, without attempting to distinguish in any way between different patterns of reactions. In a summary of the literature on this concept, Malmo (1959) describes several ways that level of activation has been measured. During deep sleep, large low-frequency brain waves appear in the EEG record, and as the person awakens and becomes active and alert, higher frequency waves appear in the EEG tracing and greater irregularity is noted. This suggests that EEG patterns may be used as a measure of level of activation. Malmo notes that muscle tension, skin resistance, heart rate, and respiration rate have also been used by different investigators as indices of level of activation. Diethelm and his co-workers (1950) have reported that degree of intensity of anxiety can be estimated by measuring decreased retention ability and slower learning on maze tests, as well as the level of epinephrine—like substances in the blood of the subjects. If further research can show that these measures are reliable indices of intensity, an important tool of investigation will be available.

Persistence

In general, the data concerning the emotions have been gathered from two sources: experimental laboratory work on animals and humans and clinical experience with human beings suffering emotional disorders. Cannon's work (1939) and Young's summary of the literature (1943) are typical of the former approach, while Dunbar's book (1947) is typical of the latter.

The laboratory studies of emotion generally induce some kind of emotion in a "normal" subject by using disturbing stimuli, such as electrical shocks, loud noises, sudden falls, or certain kinds of pictures. Introspective reports are then related to overt behavior and/or physiological changes. The study then draws conclusions about the physiological basis of fear, anger, startle, and so on.

On the other hand, the clinical studies usually examine a patient who has been anxious or depressed for a long time and then try to determine the physiological changes which have already taken place or which take place when stressful aspects of the patient's life are discussed (Wolff, 1950).

Obviously the kinds of emotions called by the same name in the two kinds of subjects and situations are not identical. Anger induced in a normal subject which is completely expressed in a few minutes or less (Ax, 1953) is not the same thing as the chronic resentment which Wolff's peptic ulcer patient showed. In general, the results of such studies will not be identical. Mahl (1952, 1953) has provided some evidence to indicate at least one difference between acute and chronic fear. He reports that in dogs and monkeys hydrochloric acid secretion increases only during chronic fear and not during acute fear. Psychiatric studies during World War II have found that soldiers who broke down early in combat displayed markedly different symptoms than those who broke down only after long combat stress (Davis, 1956). The work of Selye (1950) on the general adaptation syndrome has provided evidence to indicate that the particular character of physiological changes which are due to stress depends upon the amount of time during which any stress-provoking agent is applied. Similarly it has been shown by Babkin (1950) that increasing the number of electrical stimulations of the suprarenal gland of the cat produces a steady decline in the proportion of adrenalin secreted. Considering the importance of adrenalin in the production of the symptoms of emotion, this would again suggest that the chronic emotional state may differ quite markedly from the acute one.

Studies of emotional behavior in chimpanzees (Bindra, 1955) have reported that the initial reaction to strange stimuli (such as grotesque masks) is one of generalized excitement and marked autonomic activity, but that repeated exposure to the stimulus gradually produced well-organized patterns of response which the experimenter labeled as fear, aggression, or friendliness. This implies that long-term exposure to an emotion-provoking stimulus very likely produces different patterns of reaction than do brief exposures.

If so, some estimate of the persistence of the emotional state should be obtained for experiments to be compared meaningfully and much more research should be done on this problem. One group of investigators in psychosomatic medicine (Diethelm et al., 1950) puts the issue this way: "Studies in physiology have established the fact that the effect of emotions on some physiologic functions is far less immediate than is usually assumed by investigators. It is not known either at what point of the development of emotional reactions the physiological effects become demonstrable, or how soon they disappear in the decreasing emotion or after cessation."

Purity

In the laboratory study using normal persons, the emotions produced are usually quickly over and relatively pure. Anger, for instance, can be expressed without much fear of punishment. On the other hand in the clinical situation, many patients have conflicts about expressing their emotions, and, in addition, usually experience several at the same time. Sadness may be accompanied by anxiety, resentment, and hopelessness. Psychotherapy of depressed patients almost invariably uncovers much aggression which has been directed against the self, through fear of punishment or fear of loss of love. Hostile and aggressive behavior is often found associated with high anxiety. Thus it is evident that clinical studies seldom deal with pure emotions. Even a cursory examination of the clinical literature will indicate the difficulty of specifying the relative proportion of mixed emotions present in any given patient. Thus the relations between physiology (or life stresses) and emotions are difficult to determine. This lends a certain element of ambiguity to the conclusions of many research studies.

It would obviously be important to be able to include in reports some estimate of the kinds and proportions of emotions which act simultaneously in any patient or subject.

Individual Differences

The usual laboratory study of emotion, or of any other psychological area tacitly assumes that if the stimulus conditions are equal for all subjects then the average of all subjects' responses best represents the group for the variable being measured. This in turn implies that the subjects have equivalent life histories, an impossible assumption for studies with humans. Actually there is good reason to believe that subjects as responders in the laboratory stress situation fall into discrete classes. A study by Funkenstein et al. (1957) has shown that randomly selected college students subjected to a stress situation had at least two characteristic ways of expressing anger, some directing it outward, others toward themselves. The self-directed anger of the latter group was accompanied by anxiety. There are corresponding decreases in heart rate for one group and increases for the other. In such a case, a simple average of the responses for a group of subjects would be misleading because it would imply no *average* change of heart rate during the stress, whereas in reality almost all subjects reacted strongly.

This same kind of effect has often been reported in drug studies. For example, Phillips (1956) writes: "If the effect of drugs in terms of group statistics is to shift the group toward more active behavior patterns, isolated individuals may yet become even quieter. . . . reactions to certain drugs may be bewilderingly diverse; we all know the paranoid, as well as the belligerent, or the depressed, or elated reactions to alcohol. There are differences even within the same individual in such reactions, depending on the circumstances or the amount of intake." This implies that the data obtained from the various subgroups should be treated as a unit, but separately from the overall averages.

The problem of individual differences in response to standardized situations has occasionally been discussed in the literature under the heading of the law of initial values. This means simply that the magnitude of the response an individual gives to a standard stressor depends not only on the intensity of stimulation but also on the initial prestimulus level.

A study by Bridger and Reiser (1959) illustrates this very interestingly. Twenty-five infants were repeatedly stimulated by an air puff or by warm or cold water while heart rates were continuously recorded. It was found that each infant might show either a heart rate increase or decrease to the same stimulus depending on what the heart rate happened to be when the stimulus was applied. For example, in one case, if the heart rate was initially below 120 beats per minute, stimulation produced an increase in rate, while if the heart rate was initially above 120 beats per minute, stimulation produced a decrease in rate. This phenomenon, sometimes described as paradoxical, is subsumed under the law of initial values (Wilder, 1957). A summary of some of the recent literature dealing with this problem is given by Plutchik (1958).

These various reports imply that studies of emotion are very likely to find individual differences, "paradoxical" physiological reactions, and subgroups of subjects. These factors must be evaluated if research is to be meaningfully interpreted.

Introspection

There has been a great deal of concern in theories of emotion with the problem of introspective reports, or what

might be called the feeling of emotion. The early con-
troversies over the James-Lange theory were mostly concerned with where the *feeling* of the emotion was to be
placed, when the whole sequence of events is considered
which might be related to emotions. The usual common-
sense notion of the sequence is *perception* of a situation,
feeling of an emotion, and then *action*, either overt or
internal or both. The James-Lange theory tried to change
this sequence to perception, action, feeling. The recent
theory of Bull and Gidro-Frank (1950) suggests that the
sequence is perception, preparation, feeling, action. But
all of the theories have at least this much in common, that
in the definition of emotion, the feeling plays a necessary
role.

There are four important issues connected with this
problem of feelings in emotion. First, the evidence on
which this kind of theory is based stems largely from the
laboratory studies of pure, momentary emotions and not
from the persistent mixed emotions of clinical experience.
A person whose emotions center around simultaneous and
persistent resentment and anxiety cannot have his emotional state fitted neatly into the paradigms suggested
above.

The second major problem in this connection is that
many emotional states are not conscious. If repression is a
fact, and there is good reason to believe it is, it is exactly
this feeling of an experienced emotion that the individual
is repressing. This is a commonplace in clinical practice.
Often a fair amount of treatment is required before the
patient recognizes the feelings he may have of hostility,
anxiety, sadness, longing, and so on. Saul has suggested
(1939) that repression may vary in degree and that this
affects the development of psychosomatic symptoms, a
fact demonstrated by Frankle (1952). Lacey and Smith
(1954) have been able to study the conditioning of unconscious (presumably repressed) anxiety in the laboratory.

Thirdly, many studies are done with lower animals. If
these experiments are to be considered valid (and more

than one current theory utilizes this kind of information), then introspections cannot be crucial.

And finally, even when introspections are possible, there is serious question about the reliability and meaningfulness of the verbal report. In the history of psychology, it has been pointed out many times that introspecting about our own emotions often changes them. "Partly as a consequence of this, accounts of emotion by trained, dedicated introspectionists become progressively more impoverished, dwindling from Wundt's tridimensional account to the unidimensional description by Titchener, to Nafe's meagre discrimination of bright and dull pressures in the midregion of the body" (Farber and West, 1960). Even more serious is Young's conclusion (1927) about the method of introspection: "Some of the conditions which determine the report in affective psychology are (a) the observer's education in psychology which includes the kind and the amount of his information; (b) the observer's bias determined in part by his theoretical reflections; (c) the observer's understanding of words and his habits of speech; and (d) the suggestions which happen to reach him from various sources."

These four points, that is, the existence of mixed and repressed emotions, the use of animals and infants in research on emotion, and the unreliability of introspection as an exclusive method of investigation, imply very strongly that the subjective feelings associated with emotion should not be a *necessary* part of the definition of an emotion. Since this is the case, how then should emotions be conceived? This raises the question of definition.

Definition

The following chapter analyzes various definitions of emotion; at this point only some general comments will be made.

An ideal definition of emotion requires a statement of the necessary and sufficient conditions for applying the term. A necessary condition is one without which the emotion cannot be said to have occurred. A sufficient condition is one which enables us to apply the word emotion but is only one reason or condition among many. If a necessary condition cannot be determined, then it is adequate to specify the various sufficient conditions (reduction statements) which make the term applicable.

Since an individual may "have" an emotion and not be aware of it, then feelings may be a sufficient condition but not a necessary one. Also certain physiological changes, like a rapidly beating heart due to exercise, may exist without the individual's being in an emotional state. Thus though physiological changes may be necessary for an emotion, they are clearly not sufficient. (Some physiological changes, such as those resulting from an injection of adrenalin, may be sufficient to produce an emotional state.)

Somehow the necessary and sufficient conditions for using the word emotion have to be determined so that they do not require introspections, they can be applied to lower animals, they can be applied to mixed or pure emotions, and they can be applied to emotions of varying intensity and persistence.

One advance would be to determine certain biological functions which fit these criteria. These functions will probably include certain chemical or neurological changes that take place within the organism. They will also include certain overt patterns which go with the expression of the emotion, and certain covert patterns which go with the repression of the emotion. In other words, an individual who tries to repress the overt manifestations of anger will develop certain covert patterns of muscular tension (Plutchik, 1954), as well as certain modifications of internal functioning (Wolff, 1950). These changes in the body which result from repression of an emotion may be conceived of as conceptually equivalent to the symptoms of the emotion in its expressed form.

This implies the need for a concept of emotions as idealized states in somewhat the same way that the physicist conceptualizes the point masses, freely falling bodies, and frictionless surfaces to which his laws, strictly speaking, apply. The psychologist's task, like the physicist's, is to show why reality does not approximate the definition, not vice versa.

"Pure" emotions, in this ideal sense, may be defined by various properties which can be approached experimentally only by a series of successive approximations, as the different variables which affect the measurement of the emotion are eliminated or kept constant. It is only through a recognition of what these variables are that an effective experimental program can be instituted.

This chapter has pointed out some of the major reasons for the persisting disagreements in the study of emotion. One of the major reasons is that the intensity of the emotions studied has seldom been specified; another that the degree of persistence of the emotional state is often unknown; a third that most, if not all, of the emotions encountered in daily life and in laboratory or clinic situations are mixed emotions rather than pure. Each of these factors are now known to affect the results obtained from experiments. Another area of disagreement is due to the extensive individual differences found in research, a fact not taken into adequate consideration. Still other difficulties develop because some experimenters rely exclusively on introspective reports while others study infants or lower animals. Different definitions of emotion are implicit in these different approaches. Finally it was noted that emotions should be defined as hypothetical constructs or ideal states whose properties can be approached only gradually by a series of successive approximations.

3

Contemporary Theories of Emotion: A Review

Unless we take an extremely pessimistic view of human life, we might well say that such "pleasurable emotions" or "positive emotions" are, in general, just as numerous and important in human life as are the "unpleasurable" or "negative" emotions. It is hard to see, therefore, why they secure merely passive mention and why such emotions as fear and anger are discussed as though they are the only valid prototypes of emotion.

—ROBERT LEEPER

The history of psychology is so marked with differences as to the meaning of emotion that some psychologists have suggested that the term be eliminated from psychological writings. So far these attempts have been unsuccessful. Emotion reappears under such pseudonyms as stress, frustration, conflict, or avoidance tendency.

The study of emotions has at least three general aspects: 1) the concern with feeling states or introspections; 2) the concern with behavior or overt expression, and 3) the concern with physiology or neurology. The different theories of emotion that have been developed usually focus on one or another of these aspects.

Another way in which theories may be said to differ is in terms of the questions they attempt to answer. Chapter 1 contains a list of relevant questions about emotion; various theories direct their attention toward different questions, so much so that there is often little overlap between them. Some of the theories are actually little more than definitions of emotion.

Finally, it may be noted that many authors focus on only one or two emotions and write as if the word emotion denotes a single unitary phenomenon, as if "pleasure-seeking and melancholia, mother-love and temper tantrums, (belong) always in the same single category called emotion" (Hebb, 1949). A theory of anxiety, for example, is not the same as a theory of emotion. An adequate theory must be able to integrate meaningfully not only anger and fear, but joy and pride, curiosity and disgust, and in general, the wide gamut of emotions which are considered to be part of everyday experiences.

Some of the contemporary theories of emotion will be evaluated in the remaining part of this chapter. Most of the theories developed as an attempt to solve different problems.

James-Lange Theory

The classic theory in the field is the formulation of William James, who, in 1884, stated that ". . . bodily changes follow directly the *perception* of the exciting fact, and our feelings of the same changes as they occur *is* the emotion." It is clear from his writings that he conceived of his theory largely to answer the question *What comes first in emotion, the feeling or the bodily changes?* His answer has been challenged and defended by many psychologists since that time, but a definite answer to the question is still lacking. In fact, Lindsley, in his 1950 article on emotion in the *Handbook of Experimental Psychology*, writes, "It appears that the James-Lange theory, by its very nature and formulation, is not a theory but an untestable hypothesis." If we think of it also in terms of the list of questions in the first chapter of this book, we note that most of them are unanswered. For example, what does the theory say about the functions of emotion or what produces them, or the effects of learning, or the relation to maladjustment, or the question of differences between them? Magda Arnold (1960) has particularly emphasized that the theory does not deal with the basic question of how a perception can produce either a felt emotion *or* a bodily upset.

In addition, the formulation does not deal at all with the problem of acute versus persistent emotions, nor with the question of repressed emotions, i.e., emotions one is unaware of. This last possibility would be meaningless in James' terms and yet emotions without awareness are a commonplace of clinical practice. In this connection it is of interest that Freud made one comment on the James-Lange theory in his published writings, to wit, "what psychology has to say about affects—the James-Lange theory, for instance—is utterly incomprehensible to us psychoanalysts and impossible for us to discuss" (1953). Golightly (1953) has pointed out that although this theory has had an important influence in the history of psychology, the theory is now generally abandoned. He infers this partly from the fact that "whereas 16 of 34 contributors to the First International Symposium on Feelings and Emotions held in 1928 made some reference to the James-Lange theory, only two of 47 contributors to the Second Symposium held in 1950 did so." From the point of view of the various problems discussed earlier, the theory even if "true" would be of very limited generality since it is concerned with introspective states of feeling obtainable only in human adults. James was limited by the psychology of his era to assuming that only introspective observation could provide the basis for a psychology of emotion.

Attitude Theory

Within the last few years, a theory of emotion has been proposed by Nina Bull, the so-called Attitude theory of emotion, which has certain similarities to the James-Lange hypothesis. In the author's words:

> The fundamental concept in the theory is that feeling or affect is dependent on preparatory motor attitude —and hence that attitude is essential to emotion . . . Emotion is conceived of as a sequence of neuro-muscular events in which a postural set or preparatory motor attitude is the initial step. This preparatory attitude is both involuntary and instinctive and is the end-result of a slight, tentative movement which gives a new orientation to the individual, but does not im-mediately go into the consummatory stage of action (1952).

In an earlier paper, she had noted that the difference between this and the James-Lange theory, for example, is that "the sorry feeling comes with readiness to cry, and not because of actual crying. . . . Violent crying elimi-nates the sorry feeling" (1945).

In two ingenious studies (Bull and Gidro-Frank, 1950, Pasquarelli and Bull, 1951), Bull and her co-workers, using hypnotized subjects, found consistent bodily sensations re-ported when certain emotion words such as fear, anger, disgust, triumph, or depression were suggested. Later when other subjects were asked to "lock" their postures into certain positions, again under hypnosis, they could not change feeling unless their positions were also changed. From these findings, they drew two important conclusions: first, that skeletal muscle activity as well as visceral activ-ity is involved in emotional feeling, and second, that dif-ferent emotions not only feel different but have different postural sets associated with them.

The theory as Bull developed it resembles a position elaborated only briefly by Claparède in the Wittenberg Symposium on Emotion in 1928. He presented the follow-ing scheme (the arrows meaning leads to or is followed by):

Classic Theory: Perception → Emotion → Organic Re-actions.

James-Lange Theory: Perception → Organic Reactions → Emotions.

Modified Peripheral Theory: Perception → Attitude (of flight) → Feeling (of danger) → Organic Reactions → Emotions.

Flight Without Emotion: Perception → Attitude (of flight) → Feeling (of danger) → Flight.

This view obviously distinguishes between feelings and emotions, a dichotomy characterized by persisting disagreements and ambiguities.

The Attitude theory is still concerned with the basic problem of sequence and has relatively little to say about most of the other questions raised earlier. It still falls within the introspective tradition in psychology and thus has limited usefulness for a broad conception of the emotions.

Another point of view which falls within the introspective tradition has been advanced by Arnold (1960). She notes that one of the key problems overlooked by most theorists is the question of how a perception of a situation can lead either to a felt emotion or a bodily change. She concludes that before a situation can be effective in producing an emotional reaction of any type, it must somehow be evaluated. With this as a basis, she arrives at the following definition: emotion is "the felt tendency toward anything intuitively appraised as good (beneficial), or away from anything intuitively appraised as bad (harmful). This attraction or aversion is accompanied by a pattern of physiological changes organized toward approach or withdrawal. The patterns differ for different emotions."

Arnold suggests as an hypothesis that lower animals too are capable of immediate estimates of things as harmful or beneficial and thus provides some basis for generalizing her definition. On the other hand, no analysis is made of the fact that many different emotions exist, such as grief, surprise, disgust, and so on which are not all simply approach or avoidance reactions. Also most of the other questions for a theory are not incorporated.

Cannon-Bard Theory

The Cannon-Bard theory has achieved considerable prominence in the analysis of emotions. In the words of one of the authors, "when (thalamic) neurones discharge in a particular combination they not only innervate muscles and viscera but also excite afferent paths to the cortex . . . The peculiar quality of the emotion is added to simple sensation when the thalamic processes are roused" (1927). The evidence for this belief has been obtained mainly through electrical stimulation studies of the thalamus in cats, which produces so-called emotional behavior, and through studies of decorticate cats. Such cats, after recovery from the effects of the operation, show sham rage or fear and are capable of being sexually aroused.

The conception of the thalamus as the center of the emotions has been criticized by many authors (Hebb, 1949, Arnold, 1960). Masserman, for example (1950), has noted that the motor effects of electrical stimulation of the thalamus are only partially similar to those observed naturally. They differ in not being directed at objects in the environment and they stop abruptly when the stimulus ceases. It has also been shown (Meyers, 1950) that stimulation of other areas of the brain produces emotional behavior and that emotional expressions are obtainable even when most of the hypothalamus has been destroyed. Meyers concludes that there are three basic fallacies underlying the notion of the thalamus as the center of emotion: "1) that of imputing to one agent what may in fact be ascribable to many; 2) that of assuming that because one agent plays thus and such a role, another cannot or does not; and 3) that of supposing that the behavior of an organism is phenomenologically divisible into two distinct classes—'intellectual' and 'emotional.' "

There is another important point that might be raised in connection with the thalamic theory as described: it still stems from an introspectionist orientation and is basically concerned with the neural structure somehow associated with feeling states. Even if we knew all the neural structures involved in emotional expression, this would still not provide an answer to many of the questions raised earlier, such questions, for example, as the nature of repression and control of emotions, the persistence and mixing of emotions, and so on. Freud's comment is especially relevant here: "Today I must say I know of nothing less important for the psychological comprehension of anxiety than a knowledge of the nerve-paths by which the excitations travel" (1953).

Activation Theory

A theory which has been called the Activation theory of emotion has been mainly developed by Schlosberg (1954). "Instead of treating emotion as a special state, differing qualitatively from other states, the theory locates emotional behavior on a continuum that includes all behavior. This continuum, general level of activation, has its low end in sleep, its middle ranges in alert attention, and its high end in the strong emotions." In addition to this intensity dimension two qualitative dimensions are added: pleasantness-unpleasantness, and attention-rejection. These three dimensions of emotion are conceptualized by a cone-shaped model with a roughly circular horizontal cross-section depicting the two qualitative axes, while the vertical dimension represents the intensity dimension. Thus far, the only experimental work based on the model concerns the judgment of facial expressions from photographs using the two qualitative axes, and the effect of level of activation on certain simple motor tasks as well as some physiological measures.

This theory is an important advance over the previous ones in that it does attempt to integrate into a single model several recognized dimensions of emotion; it also includes pleasant as well as unpleasant feelings. It does not, however, explicitly comment on a number of important issues which have been raised here. For example, what is the difference between acute and chronic emotion in this theory? What is meant by repression of emotion?

What produces emotion? What *is* an emotion, and so on? It is quite possible, of course, that the answers to these questions can eventually be made explicit by the theory—this in fact could be true of any of the theories already described—but these questions have not received an explicit answer as yet.

Motivational Theory

A few years ago Leeper (1948) published an article in which he advocated a motivational definition of emotion to replace the definition of emotion as a disorganized response. He pointed out that the most common definition of emotion is exemplified by Young's description (1943), "an acute disturbance of the individual as a whole, psychological in origin, involving behavior, conscious experience, and visceral functioning." Leeper showed a number of contradictions in the previous uses of the term disorganization and finally suggested a specific definition, to wit: "The criterion of organization, consequently, is not a matter of whether there is some interference with preceding activities. It is the question whether this interference is relatively chaotic and haphazard, or whether the suppressions and changes of subordinate activities are harmonious with some main function which is being served."

Based on this definition, emotions can be conceived of primarily as motives because they are processes which arouse, sustain, and direct activity. The physiological and behavioral changes that occur during emotions may be different from previous states, but they help the individual prepare for, or do what is necessary at the moment.

This conception is, in certain respects, consistent with the idea that emotions represent emergency reactions of fight or flight in that the preparations for such energetic activity is highly organized from a physiological point of view, even though preceding activities such as digestion or intellectual activity may be modified or temporarily stopped. Leeper's main point of disagreement with the emergency theory is that he insists that pleasurable emo-

tions such as joy, love, and delight do not represent emergency reactions, but that they still must be included within
the framework of a theory.

This emphasis on emotion as organized is a useful antidote to earlier rationalistic speculations which conceived of
emotion only as interfering with activities. However as
Hebb (1949) points out, the result of Leeper's argument
is to broaden the category of emotion so much that it
includes all psychological processes because almost all act
to "arouse, sustain, and direct" behavior. Hebb suggests
as an alternative view that emotion be regarded not as a
single, unitary process, but in dualistic terms: *integrative*
emotions are those in which there is a tendency to maintain or increase the original stimulating conditions, while
disintegrative emotions are those in which the tendency is
to abolish or decrease the stimulus.

Although this problem of organization in emotions is an
important one, it is still too narrow to qualify as an adequate theory of emotions. Many other important problems
concerned with the effects of learning, the nature of pat-
terning, the nature of repression and control are left unanswered. An important issue has been touched but a comprehensive theory is still needed.

Psychoanalytic Theory

Perhaps the most comprehensive and influential theory
of personality today is psychoanalytic theory. Even a
casual acquaintance with the literature indicates that psychoanalytic theory is concerned not only with personality,
but with emotions as well, and particularly the emotion of
anxiety. In psychoanalysis there are many implications for
a theory of emotions, although as Ostow (1959) notes:
"There is no systematic treatment of affect as a category
in psychoanalytic theory." This same point is made by
Zangwill (1948) when he writes: "Neither [Freud] nor
any of his followers have devoted any systematic attention
to the problem of emotion in general."

One attempt at developing the basis for a psychoanalytic

theory of emotion has been made by Rapaport (1950). Rapaport quotes Freud (1925) as saying that "affects and emotions correspond with processes of discharge, the final expression of which is perceived as feeling. In the present state of our knowledge of affects and emotions we cannot express this difference more clearly." Those investigators who seek to establish clear-cut relations between emotion felt and bodily processes are bound to fail because "the dynamics of psychic manifestations are *unconscious,* and cannot be found by investigating interrelations of the data of physiology and the data of consciousness."

The old source of controversy between the James-Lange and the Cannon-Bard theories is essentially dismissed by pointing out that in the psychoanalytic theory a percept will elicit unconscious processes which may be followed in any sequence by the bodily process, by the emotion felt, by only one of these, or by neither, for both are conceived of as manifestations of the same psychic process. Emotion as well as thought, according to Freud's theorizing (1925), is experimenting at action with small amounts of energy.

The following main elements according to Rapaport (1950) are assumed in the psychoanalytic view: a) that an unconscious process occurs between the perception of the stimulus evoking emotion and the peripheral physiological process; b) that the peripheral physiological process and the emotion felt are both discharge processes of the same instinctual source of energy; c) that emotions are expressions of instinctual conflict; and d) that momentary manifestations of emotion should be differentiated from chronic.

This theory, as far as it goes, makes some important contributions. It eliminates the sequence problem (i.e., which came first, the feeling or the bodily change), an issue which has proved a stumbling block for over fifty years; it emphasizes that emotional processes are unconscious and cannot, therefore, be examined by introspection alone. By implication, these processes must be inferred in human beings, just as we infer emotional processes in lower animals. It suggests that conflicts are involved in emotion and recognizes the problem of persistence.

The main weaknesses of the theory are its vagueness and metaphorical character and the fact that certain basic questions remain unanswered. For example, what does it mean to control our emotions, how do the emotions of infants differ from those of adults, what are the stimuli which produce emotion, are there differences between emotions, and so on? There is also the possibility that different analysts have somewhat different conceptions about the nature of emotions; there is no unanimity as yet, nor was there in Freud's own writings. There is still adequate opportunity for development of these conceptions.

Many other psychoanalysts have written about emotions either from the point of view of the conditions which bring them about or from the point of view of their consequences. These contributions are too numerous to be adequately summarized briefly and they will therefore be integrated where appropriate with other material in the subsequent chapters.

Behavioristic Theories

The development of behaviorism was associated with an attempt on the part of the leading proponents to apply the concepts of this school of thought to many of the traditional problems of psychology, including the problem of the nature of emotions. Although many writers have dealt with one or another aspect of emotion or a particular emotion such as anxiety, from this point of view few have attempted to discuss the general nature of emotion. Among the few who have are Watson, Tolman, and Skinner and this summary will therefore be limited to their views.

WATSON

In 1924, Watson in his *Psychology from the Standpoint of a Behaviorist* defined emotion as "an hereditary pattern-reaction involving profound changes of the bodily mechanism as a whole, but particularly of the visceral and glandular systems." He then defined "pattern-reaction" as meaning that "the separate details of response appear with some constancy, with some regularity and in approximately the same sequential order each time the exciting stimulus is presented."

This view, as developed, implied that emotion is always disruptive of organized activity and that the basic pattern of emotional reaction is unlearned. Learning or conditioning enters into the picture to "break-up" and partially inhibit the expression of the hereditary pattern of emotion, although he noted that only the external features of the primitive pattern can be inhibited and that the visceral and glandular aspects of the pattern remain. Watson also distinguished between pattern-type of reaction and activity level, the former implying a distinction between anger and grief, for example, and the latter implying a general intensity dimension. This general orientation led Watson to try to determine the simple stimuli which arouse patterns of emotional reaction in newborn infants, with the result that he reported three basic patterns he called x, y, and z but which resembled reactions called fear, rage, and love in adults.

Consistent with his behavioral view, Watson did not attempt a physiological or neural analysis of emotion but instead pointed out that "it is perfectly possible for a student of behavior entirely ignorant of the sympathetic nervous system and of the glands and smooth muscles, or even of the central nervous system as a whole, to write a thoroughly comprehensive and accurate study of the emotions —the types, their interrelations with habits, their role, etc." Unfortunately the behavioristic program implied here has never been systematically carried out.

Watson's view is one which clearly conceives of emotion in somewhat the same way an unconditioned response is defined, i.e., as a group of responses which occur with some constancy and regularity to a given stimulus. His distinction between pattern-type and activity level important though it is has received systematic attention only in recent years. The major limitation is that the ideas are not developed to answer the various kinds of questions already posed.

TOLMAN

The analysis of emotion developed by Tolman is more subtle than Watson's and more specific. He begins by raising the basic problem of how to identify emotion in infants and lower animals and concludes that this poses the question of how we learn to apply emotion words to ourselves as children, or even as adults.

When a person says that he is angry, this does not tell us what his conscious state is, which we can never know directly, but only that he is in a condition which makes him likely to behave in a certain way, a way which is related to the conditions under which he learned to use the word angry in the first place. Interestingly enough, Tolman indicates that emotion is not the exhibited behavior which a person shows, but rather the "*readiness or drive* for such behavior," thus implying that emotion is some kind of an hypothetical state.

Tolman emphasizes that emotion cannot be defined by responses alone or by stimuli alone but only in terms of the relations between the two. In emotion, the responses of the organism are designed to affect or change the stimulus situation. For example, in fear, most of the responses may be thought of as acting to *protect* the individual in some way; in anger, most of the responses act to *destroy* the stimulus. Emotions, therefore, may be defined "as a *drive* or *tendency* toward a particular type of behavior result, of *response-as-affecting-stimulus*; e.g., in the case of fear, protection from the stimulus, in the case of anger, destruction of the stimulus, and in the case of love, encouragement or enticement of the stimulus" (Tolman, 1923). Tolman makes no attempt in the course of the analysis to discuss such questions as the effect of learning on emotion, the repression of emotion, the genetic development of emotion, and so on. The major value of his paper is in providing an approach to a definition of emotion applicable to adults, infants, and lower animals, thus enabling the possibility of development of a general theory.

SKINNER

Skinner's views of emotion are presented mainly in two sources, *The Behavior of Organisms* (1938) and *Science and Human Behavior* (1953). In the earlier work he points out that "emotion is not primarily a kind of response at all but rather a state of strength comparable in many respects with a drive." The way an individual judges the existence of emotion in another person is not by checking his blood pressure or level of adrenalin but simply by observing changes in the appearance of certain learned responses, such as rate of talking or overall approach or avoidance. There are, however, certain stimuli or operations which he calls emotional because they produce an emotional state. He lists four types: 1) unconditioned stimuli such as shock, 2) restraint of a response, 3) withholding of a reinforcement, and 4) certain drugs. There is no attempt made to distinguish between different emotions.

In his later book, Skinner notes that emotions are often described as causes of behavior. (We often say that a man runs away because of fear or strikes because of anger.) Skinner finds this view inadequate. "A man does not neglect his business *because* of anxiety or worry . . . The only valid cause is the external condition of which the behavior of neglect . . . [is] . . . a function."

On the other hand, Skinner is apparently willing to retain the concept of emotion as some kind of an hypothetical state which represents a disposition to act in a certain way. He defines emotion as "a particular state of strength or weakness in one or more responses induced by any one of a class of operations. We may make as many distinctions as we wish between separate emotions."

These views of emotion as developed by Skinner are unfortunately limited. Little attempt is made to specify the kinds of responses or operations connected with different emotions such as joy, fear, or sorrow. He does not explain why all behavior should not be considered emotional though all behavior can be changed in strength by suitable reinforcement operations. Almost all of the questions raised in Chapter 1 are left untouched.

The major value of the behavioristic definitions of emotion is the general nature of the approach which makes the concept applicable to all organismic levels. The focusing on overt behavior also provides a useful contrast with those views which somehow seek to localize emotion in some part of the nervous system or those views which focus only on feeling states.

On the other hand, any attempt to study isolated responses as such will not likely lead to a fruitful increase in our understanding of emotion. Hebb, for example, has reported the results of a two-year study of chimpanzee behavior which carefully attempted to avoid anthropomorphic description (1946).

> A formal experiment was set up to provide records of the actual behavior of the adult chimpanzees, and from these records to get an objective statement of the differences from animal to animal. All that resulted was an almost endless series of specific acts in which no order or meaning could be found. On the other hand, by the use of frankly anthropomorphic concepts of emotion and attitude one could quickly and easily describe the peculiarities of the individual animals.

The preceding pages have briefly outlined seven different approaches to a theory of emotion. Each approach deals with some important problem and yet leaves others unanswered. Some of these theories remain in our textbooks despite contradictory facts or relevant criticism. This is probably due to the nature of the scientific process, for as Conant (1947) has noted, a theory is never overthrown by contradictory facts; it is only overthrown by a better theory.

In the following chapters a theory of emotion will be presented which attempts to deal with the issues already raised. It utilizes ideas taken from various sources and disciplines and attempts a new integration.

4

Basic Postulates of the Theory

Scientific as well as cultural trends seem to progress by way of thesis and antithesis to eventual synthesis.

—MAGDA ARNOLD

In presenting a new organization of the data, it is difficult, if not impossible, to trace each of the psychological steps involved in arriving at these ideas. What is offered here is only the most recent stage of development of an evolving conception and is, in essence, a rational reconstruction of various formulations and stages of thinking.

In any scientific discipline, theories are designed to include a wide range of facts or observations in the simplest possible framework. In the history of science, it has become clear that theories, unlike facts, cannot be conceived of as true or false, but only as useful or not useful. Newton's theories are not considered untrue but simply less applicable to certain limiting conditions than Einstein's. In atomic physics today and recently in the application of mathematics to learning problems, several different theories have been proposed with widely different conceptual bases but all leading to approximately the same deductions.

The theory of emotion presented here utilizes all of the procedures described in Chapter 1. It attempts both an analysis and a synthesis of the complex emotions of everyday life; it conceives of the units of analysis as ideal cases or hypothetical constructs, and it proceeds by analogy. It is hoped that the theory will be judged in terms of its usefulness in explaining old observations, suggesting new ones, and relating diverse ideas. This chapter will present the basic postulates of the theory along with a summary of the kind of historical background and reasoning that led to each postulate. These comments should not be thought of as "proof" of the postulates but only as heuristic devices designed to make them seem plausible. The theory itself should be evaluated as a total conception having utility in relating general psychological, clinical, and biological observations within a common framework.

Postulates of the Present Theory

Postulate 1. There is a small number of pure or primary emotions.

Postulate 2. All other emotions are mixed; that is, they can be synthesized by various combinations of the primary emotions.

Postulate 3. Primary emotions differ from each other with regard to both physiology and behavior.

Postulate 4. Primary emotions in their pure form are hypothetical constructs or idealized states

whose properties can only be inferred from
various kinds of evidence.

Postulate 5.   Primary emotions may be conceptualized in
terms of pairs of polar opposites.

Postulate 6.   Each emotion can exist in varying degrees
of intensity or levels of arousal.

The following sections will comment upon each of the
postulates. Because of the close interrelation between the
first two postulates, they will be discussed together.

POSTULATE 1.   *There is a small number of pure or
primary emotions.*

POSTULATE 2.   *All other emotions are mixed; that is,
they can be synthesized by various
combinations of the primary emotions.*

The concept of primary and secondary emotions has a
long history in the literature of philosophy. Descartes
assumed that there were only six primary emotions or,
as he called them, passions, and that all others were composed of mixtures of these six or derived from them. He
suggested that love, hatred, desire, joy, sadness, and admiration were primary emotions but gave no justification
for his choice.

A far more extensive attempt to develop a system of
the emotions was presented by Spinoza, who assumed only
three primary affects, "joy, sorrow, and desire"; all others
were assumed to spring from these. For example, he
wrote, "Love is nothing but joy accompanied with the
idea of an external cause, and hatred is nothing but sorrow
with the accompanying idea of an external cause." Fear
was described as "an unsteady sorrow, arising from the
image of a doubtful thing. If the doubt be removed . . .
then . . . fear becomes despair. . . . Remorse is the
sorrow which is opposed to gladness. . . . Pride is that
joy which arises from a man's thinking too much of himself." Spinoza attempted to analyze a number of common
emotions using this procedure but gave no justification
for his choice of primaries; nor is it clearly evident how

he decided on the components of a particular complex emotion.

Later Hobbes suggested that there were seven simple passions: "appetite, desire, love, aversion, hate, joy and grief," and several English philosophers of the nineteenth century continued making distinctions of a similar kind. These views were given their most extensive development by McDougall early in the twentieth century. His views are described extensively in his textbook of social psychology, 1921.

He notes that all animals including man have "instincts" or "propensities" and that when these are activated an affective quality is associated with each which we call emotion. For example, the instinct to flee from danger is associated with the emotion of fear, the instinct of pugnacity is associated with the emotion of anger, and so on. In all he assumes seven important, clearly defined instincts and five more obscure, less differentiated ones, as follows:

Instinct	*Emotion*
Flight	fear
Repulsion	disgust
Curiosity	wonder
Pugnacity	anger
Self-abasement	subjection
Self-assertion	elation
Parental	"tender"

The five less clearly defined instincts are the gregarious instinct, the acquisitive instinct, the construction instinct, the reproductive instinct, and an instinct connected with the desire for food.

The secondary or complex emotions are illustrated by such things as hate, which McDougall defines as a mixture of anger, fear, and disgust; or scorn, which is a mixture of anger and disgust; or loathing, which results from the combination of fear and disgust. Relatively few other emotions are analyzed in this way. No specific criterion is given for arriving at the components in any mixed emotion.

McDougall, however, is one of the few writers on this subject who makes some attempt to explain the methods used to decide which emotions are primary. He suggests three criteria: 1) a similar emotion and impulse is clearly shown in the behavior of the higher animals; 2) the emotion and impulse occasionally appear in humans with "morbidly exaggerated intensity" (which presumably indicates its relatively independent functioning in the mind); and 3) most of the complex emotions can be conceived of as mixtures of the primaries. Unfortunately, McDougall does not apply these criteria consistently. He refuses to accept joy and sorrow as primary emotions, even though they are occasionally expressed in the morbidly exaggerated forms of mania and depression; he arrives at components of mixtures strictly on the basis of his own introspections. In addition, his utilization of the concept of instinct, a concept which has fallen into disrepute in contemporary writing, has left many psychologists highly skeptical of the general scheme. This is, in a way, unfortunate since there are many interesting and perceptive observations to be found in his work.

This attempt by McDougall to describe behavior in terms of primary emotions is by no means the most recent such attempt. In the 1928 Wittenberg Symposium, Jörgensen proposed his own scheme. He suggested six primary emotions: "fear, happiness, sorrow, want, anger, and shyness" with the possibility that "loathing" might also be one. He noted the very important point that the naming of these primaries is partly fortuitous because they each may vary in intensity. Thus fear might also be called "dread, terror, anxiety or apprehension" and "sorrow" might be called "grief, despair, pain, or despondency." Using this scheme, he interprets "hope" as a mixture of "want, sorrow and happiness," and "envy" as a mixture of "sorrow and want." Here again, no meaningful criterion is given for deciding on the units within each mixture.

One of the most recent attempts to develop a list of basic tendencies which overlaps with the notion of primary emotions has been presented by Murray (1954). He develops a meaningful rationale for deciding on basic tendencies: "Every self-and-body, in order to develop, maintain, express and reproduce itself, must perform a number of individual roles (functions) such as respiration, ingestion of food, construction of new tissue, excretion, defense against assault and disease, expression of emotions and sentiments, copulation, and so forth." This implies that each individual develops certain dispositions or tendencies related to these functions which Murray calls rejection, acquisition, construction, retention, renunciation, expression, maintenance, elimination, bestowal, avoidance, aggression, defendance. Murray then implies (but does not adequately elaborate) that any human interaction can be expressed in terms of these basic action tendencies.

This summary of these various attempts to analyze emotions in terms of a small number of primaries indicates that there has been relatively little consistency in the past. This is most likely due to the reliance on introspections, the lack of adequate rationales for selecting the primaries, and the lack of empirical validation and implication. The idea of primary emotions is an important one with relevance to human experience, but these problems must be solved if it is to have more than historical interest. See Chapter 5 for an analysis of these problems.

POSTULATE 3. *Primary emotions differ from each other with regard to both physiology and behavior.*

It is unlikely that anyone would question the statement that emotions differ from one another introspectively, that sorrow, for example, feels different from anger. College students when asked to judge various emotions in terms of certain verbal scales overwhelmingly describe "fear" as unpleasant, tense, excited, and contracted, and "love" as pleasant, relaxed, excited, and expansive. In a study concerned with the phenomenology of emotion, Block (1957) asked students to rate fifteen emotions on twenty verbal scales. The results indicate fairly clear differences in the subjective feelings associated with each of the emotions.

Anger, for example, is described as active, tense, rough, high and angular as well as red, ferocious, strong and loud. Grief is sad, tense, cold, weak, as well as ugly, bad, and stale. Pride is high, active and clear as well as strong, full and loud. Similar patterns of differences were found for the other emotions used.

The problem of expressive differences between emotions has also been studied extensively and a large body of observations has been built up over the years. In his book on the *Expression of the Emotions in Man and Animals,* Darwin gave extensive descriptions of the differences between the various emotions as observed in different races of men, in children, and in the higher animals. For example, he observed: "With all or almost all animals, even with birds, terror causes the body to tremble. The skin becomes pale, sweat breaks out, and the hair bristles. . . . The breathing is hurried . . . The mental faculties are much disturbed. Utter prostration soon follows, and even fainting." A similarly vivid picture of grief is given by Lange (of James-Lange theory fame): ". . . Movements are made slowly, heavily, without strength, unwillingly and with exertion . . . [The] voice is weak and without resonance . . . The neck is bent, the head hangs ("bowed down" with grief) . . . The jaw may even hang open. . . . The face [has] pallor and shrunkenness. . . . The mouth grows dry, the tongue sticky, and a bitter taste ensues which it would appear, is only a consequence of the tongue's dryness. In nursing women the milk diminishes or altogether dries up." And with characteristic directness, Cannon (1929) describes the rage response as involving a "crouching body, frowning brow, firm lips, clenched or grinding teeth, growled threats, tightened fists, etc."

These descriptions are generally confirmed by clinical experience as well as everyday observations. They have also been confirmed by the several studies performed by Bull and her co-workers using hypnotically induced emotions (described briefly in Chapter 3).

In addition to these observations and reports on gross

expressive changes in different emotions, there is an extensive literature on the facial expressions which are characteristic of emotions. This problem has been studied using several different methods including posed expressions, natural expressions, laboratory-induced expressions, and partial expressions. Although the results are not entirely consistent, due to problems of nomenclature and learning, the findings show some general agreements.

For example, anger tends to be described in the following way: eyes—opened wide; eyebrows—knit together; forehead—very wrinkled, folds between the eyes; nostrils —widened, distended; mouth—lower lip tensely drawn backward and downward, teeth usually clenched tightly together, lips and jaw sometimes protruding. Fear is described as follows: eyes—widely open and staring; forehead—raised, transverse wrinkles; mouth—rectangular, rigid opening, lips somewhat depressed at corners. Sadness is drawn in these terms: eyes—half covered with upper eyelid; forehead—contracted, vertical wrinkles; mouth—depressed at corners, causing lower jaw to droop and lips to relax. A fair amount of agreement has also been obtained for other expressions, such as happiness, startle, sulkiness, and so on. Thus it appears that expressive differences between emotions have been consistently recognized. In fact, it should be emphasized that such differences provide the major cues that we use in judging emotions in other people.

Many years ago, Landis (1924) reported that facial expressions induced in college students in a variety of emotion-provoking situations could not be clearly distinguished for different emotions. Unfortunately this conclusion has been perpetuated in textbooks, despite severe criticisms both of the design method used (Murphy and Murphy, 1931) and of the statistical analysis (Davis, 1934). Using a different analysis of the data obtained by Landis, Davis was able to provide evidence that there may be a limited number of typical facial reaction-patterns.

This then raises the question of whether there are also physiological differences between emotions. It would seem that the overt expressive differences which have been noted would imply internal physiological differences as well: the pale face typical of fear implies a vasoconstriction of the blood vessels of the skin, while the reddened face associated with anger implies vasodilatation. Darwin noted that fear is associated with a "wildly beating heart" and occasionally with a voiding of excrements, while sadness is associated with "dull" eyes, pale face and slow respiration.

The notion of physiological differences between emotions seemed to be pretty much taken for granted until the researches of Cannon during the 1920's which apparently indicated that the autonomic changes observed in cats and dogs during fear and anger were the same. This led many psychologists to assume that the autonomic changes for all emotions in man were also the same, a conclusion which was by no means justified by the evidence.

Since that time, an increasing body of research has begun to show the existence of definite, physiological differences between emotions. Some of this work will be briefly reviewed here.

In the well known study of Tom, a patient with a gastric fistula, it was possible to observe the contents of the stomach while he experienced various emotions (Wolf and Wolff, 1942). When the patient felt sad and depressed the stomach became pale and flaccid and the hydrochloric acid secretion decreased below the normal level; when he felt resentment, the stomach became red and engorged with blood and hydrochloric acid secretion increased above normal. Very similar findings were reported for a sixteen-month-old child in whom a stomach fistula was made because of a congenital blockage of the esophagus (Reichsman, 1955). During periods of depression, hydrochloric acid and pepsin secretion were lowest, while they were markedly increased during periods of rage.

In a careful study of four patients with ulcerative colitis in whom the colon was operatively exposed to observation, similar findings were obtained. When the patients felt fear, the colon was pale in color and relatively slack and limp. Feelings of resentment were associated with a narrowing and shortening of the colon and with increased redness or hyperemia (Grace, Wolf, and Wolff, 1951). The authors conclude that "changes involving colonic hyperfunction, at first altogether functional and transitory, may, when unduly sustained, result in structural damage and disease." Observations on one hundred patients with irritable colon have indicated still other differences (Almy, 1951). Patients who described their problems in a hostile, defensive way showed an increase in intestinal motility with wave-like contractions, while patients who expressed helplessness and defeat showed a reduction in intestinal motility. Related observations were made during World War II; constipation was very common in Japanese prison camps while the dominant mood of the soldiers was depression. When one soldier was shot and another beaten publicly, after a minor infraction, there was an epidemic of diarrhea. Similar patterns of changes have been reported by Wolff (1950) as observable in the nose and vagina as well as in the stomach and colon. There is thus evidence for widespread organic changes, internal as well as external, associated with different emotions.

Some comment should also be made on the difference between fear and anger. In 1945, Magda Arnold gathered a good deal of physiological evidence to indicate that fear is associated with dominant action of the sympathetic system and high secretion of adrenalin, while anger is associated with parasympathetic dominance. Funkenstein (1955, 1957) and Ax (1953) showed that there are patterns of difference between experimentally induced fear and anger. In the first case, a group of college students were exposed to a stress situation and were found to respond in one of three ways: with "anger out," with anxiety, or with "anger in" (i.e., self-blame, etc.). Those students who responded to the stress with outwardly directed anger had cardiovascular reactions similar to those produced by injection of nor-adrenalin, while those who reacted with anxiety or anger-in showed an adrenalin-like type of response. Ax found similar patterns with his subjects.

It has also been noted that aggressive animals such as the lion have a relatively large secretion of nor-adrenalin, while domesticated or timid animals have a more marked secretion of adrenalin. Gellhorn summarized these findings in 1960, noting that "the mecholyl test, the vascular reactions, and the urinary excretion in the state of anger suggest a state of high excitability of the hypothalamus and a dominant secretion of nor-adrenaline. The same indicators suggest a lesser hypothalamic excitability and a dominant secretion of adrenaline in the state of fear." The report by Davis and his colleagues (1955) on autonomic responses to simple stimuli has raised the possibility of at least four basic patterns of reactivity, and probably more. It is thus likely that further research will gradually reveal the physiological patterns associated with the different emotions.

POSTULATE 4. *Primary emotions in their pure form are hypothetical constructs or idealized states whose properties can only be inferred from various kinds of evidence.*

This point has already been discussed in an earlier chapter. If emotion as a concept is to enter usefully into scientific thinking, it must be regarded as an invention or inference on the part of the psychologist. Emotion is not a thing in the sense that a chair or table is. Like numerous other terms in common use, it cannot be defined by the fundamental operation of "pointing at. . . . Emotion is an inference or a scientific construct" (Brown and Farber, 1951). These same authors point out that various other psychologists, such as Skinner, Hebb, Masserman, and Spence have all suggested that emotion be regarded as a construct or inference. Tolman (1923) and Nowlis (1956) have, too.

Most, if not all, of the emotions of daily experience are

mixed emotions and therefore it is difficult to make accurate inferences about the properties of the pure state. This, of course, is no different in essence from the problem faced by any scientist; all empirical situations have some degree of impurity or unwanted influences. The chemist gradually refines his materials; the physicist tries to eliminate the action of extraneous variables. In the same way, laboratory studies of emotion, through the use of lower animals, infants, children as well as by careful attention to the problems described in Chapter 2, will gradually enable more accurate inferences about the properties of the primary emotions.

POSTULATE 5. *Primary emotions may be conceptualized in terms of pairs of polar opposites.*

In recent years, a number of studies using factor analysis have been performed by Burt (1950), Cattell (1946), and Guilford and Zimmerman (1956) designed to identify certain hypothetical factors relating to emotions and personality. All of these factor analytic approaches attempt to reduce a set of observable but correlated traits or behaviors to a set of hypothetical but uncorrelated traits, factors, or components. These factors have been called primary factors or source traits by different authors. In most studies using factor analysis to study emotions or personality, bipolar factors are found. Guilford's fourteen dimensions of temperament are almost all bipolar; so are many of Cattell's. These dimensions include such factors as depression versus cheerfulness, agreeableness versus belligerence, and calmness versus nervousness. The activation theory described earlier also used pleasantness-unpleasantness and attention-rejection as polar dimensions. Nowlis (1956) has assumed four bipolar dimensions of mood as a result of a series of studies using self-rating adjective check lists. These dimensions are called level of activation, level of control, social orientation, and hedonic tone. Schaefer (1960) has shown that it is possible to analyze personality trait behavior ratings in terms of certain bipolar dimensions using a type of factor-analytic technique developed by Guttman (1954) called circumplex ordering. And certainly in our everyday experience, we tend to think about emotions in terms of opposites; we talk about happiness and sadness, love and hate, fear and anger. Cannon (1939) has written about the "fight or flight" opposition, and Schneirla (1959) has gathered an impressive amount of evidence to justify the view that "in *all* animals the species-typical pattern of behavior is based on biphasic, functionally opposed mechanisms insuring approach or withdrawal reactions according to whether stimuli of low or of high intensity, respectively, are in effect."

There is thus considerable evidence to suggest that emotions may be meaningfully conceived of in terms of bipolar opposites.

POSTULATE 6.   *Each emotion can exist in varying degrees of intensity or levels of arousal.*

Several authors have proposed this idea calling it by various names: degree of energy mobilization (Duffy, 1951), activation (Schlosberg, 1954), arousal (Duffy, 1957), and general activity (Guilford and Zimmerman, 1956). It seems to be a necessary dimension for describing emotion and regularly appears in most factor analyses of personality. Burt (1950), for example, has reported a general factor, which he calls emotional energy or general emotionality, and two specific bipolar factors, which he roughly interprets as pleasurable versus unpleasurable feelings and demonstrative versus inhibitive behavior. Our everyday language likewise distinguishes between degrees of emotion, such as terror, fear, and apprehension, or grief, sorrow, and feeling blue.

Malmo (1957) has provided some experimental evidence that level of arousal can be measured by muscle potential gradients and by level of palmar skin conductance. Dumas (in Freeman, 1939) has even attempted to relate the differences between emotions to differences of intensity. According to this view, all emotions involving mild excitement are pleasant; unpleasantness and disequilibrium occur only with strong emotions. Qualitative differences at the introspective level are reduced by this view to quantitative variations. There is thus ample reason to incorporate an intensity dimension into any theory designed to represent adequately the facts at our disposal about emotion.

These remarks about the postulates of the theory have been made only to make them seem reasonable, not necessarily to prove them. The theory's validity must be judged in terms of its ability to provide a meaningful organization of the data and its ability to stimulate research.

5

The Concept of Primary Emotions

> *We might do well to emulate Hughlings Jackson, who begged to be permitted to study first of all minor manifestations of epilepsy as being simpler to comprehend. If fish brains can do so much and if, in so many ways, human beings "irrationally" act as if they no longer possessed the full use of their acquisitions, perhaps we should do well to return to our ancestors if we wish to learn why we act as we do.*
>
> —WILLIAM J. TURNER

In the preceding chapter, it was shown that the concept of primary, pure, or basic emotions has a long history, although one marked by disagreements concerning both their number and type. It was suggested that these disagreements were due to reliance on introspections alone, to the lack of formal procedures for determining how mixtures are formed from primaries, and to a lack of theoretical implications suitable for research. These difficulties, which are quite formidable, must be surmounted if a meaningful concept of primary emotions is to be developed.

Criteria for Primary Emotions

Many scattered comments in the previous chapters can provide a meaningful basis for establishing criteria of primary emotions. It has been noted that all theories consider research with lower animals as relevant to an understanding of emotion; therefore, whatever is taken to be a primary emotion should be applicable, in some sense, to lower evolutionary levels. The view to be presented here would not restrict the concept of emotion only to the primate level, the mammalian level, or even the vertebrate level; emotion should be conceived of as relevant to the entire evolutionary scale. This suggests that emotion should be related to some kinds of basic, adaptive, biological processes, a point elaborated below.

A second implication is that a decision about which emotions are primary and which derived should not depend only on adult introspections, even though introspections may be useful in providing additional insights into the internal stimuli associated with certain adaptive reactions.

Third, although emotions may depend for expression on the integrated action of certain neural structures, they cannot be identified solely in terms of neural structures, for these structures change considerably in the course of evolution, and the most primitive organisms have no nervous systems at all. Thus if emotions are to be recognized at all evolutionary levels, they cannot be identified with particular body parts.

It follows that if emotions are not identified by the action of particular body parts or neural structures, then emotions must be recognizable in terms of total body reactions, that is, in terms of overall behavior. Even at the human level, it has been noted, people do not identify emotions in others by physiological means, by taking heart rate or blood pressure measurements; emotions are most easily recognized by what people do. If a man walks slowly, with head bent forward, speaks in a low monotone or hardly at all, does very little work and sits with a somewhat huddled posture, we are very likely to assume that he is sad or depressed, regardless of what he may say. Clinicians often know that a patient is angry or anxious though the patient is not aware of it or will not verbalize it. How often we tell someone *you look irritated* or *you look hurt,* or *you look happy,* on the basis of his facial expression, posture, movements, or general behavior. Thus it seems reasonable to conclude that the basic definition of emotion should be a behavioral one which does not depend on introspections or the existence of particular neural events.

One immediate problem posed by this view is that of distinguishing emotional behavior from all other kinds of behavior. As noted earlier, some psychologists have suggested that we do without the concept of emotion and think of all behavior simply in terms of changes of magnitude and direction. But this view has not received wide support; there seems to be need for some way of distinguishing certain special kinds of behavior as "emotional."

One solution, suggested by the first implication discussed above, is that emotion be related to some kinds of basic adaptive, biological processes. This criterion can provide a partial basis for distinguishing emotional behavior from other behavior.

To summarize, emotions considered primary should:

1. have relevance to basic biological adaptive processes
2. be found *in some form* at all evolutionary levels
3. not depend for their definition on particular neural structures or body parts
4. not depend for definition on introspections (although they may be used)
5. be defined primarily in terms of behavioral data (or to use Tolman's phrase, in terms of "response-as-affecting-stimulus")

It is implicit in this view that emotions are adaptive devices in the struggle for individual survival at all evolutionary levels.

Basic Types of Adaptive Behavior

In the attempt to identify basic types of adaptive behavior, it is necessary to find terms which apply to all animals so that generalizations can be made. Scott, in his book *Animal Behavior* (1958), puts the matter in the following way:

> When we compare the activities of a wider variety of species, we begin to see that certain kinds of behavior occur over and over again, and that these fall into a few general kinds of behavioral adaptations which are widely found in the animal kingdom. In doing this, we must meet a problem of language as well as that of careful description. What words can we use to say that two animals as unlike as elephants and spiders are doing similar things?

One clue to this problem is given by Murray (1954), who pointed out that the life processes of maintenance, development, reproduction, and expression require certain basic functions such as respiration, ingestion of food, excretion, defense, and so on. Similarly Turner (1957) has noted that:

> There is only a limited number of modes of dealing with danger available to the individual that have proved of general applicability exploitable in phylogeny. With respect to stimuli arising from within the organism, survival is favored by expulsion or by isolation. With respect to stimuli referring to a source of (potential) danger arising from the outer environment, survival is favored by flight, fight, submission, reversal, and vocalization, in the order of apparent phylogenetic development.

Perhaps an extension and formalization of these ideas might provide a key to the basic types of adaptive behavior we are seeking.

Such an extension has been made by Scott, who documents with a great deal of evidence the concept that there are nine general types of adaptive behavior. These are described and illustrated below and their relevance for a theory of emotion suggested.

Ingestive behavior. All organisms, in order to survive, must take in food in some form. This is as true for the amoeba as it is for man.

Shelter-seeking. An animal tends to move about until it finds conditions favorable for its existence. Even paramecia will move close to the bodies of other paramecia, forming a group. Scott suggests that "this is actually a very primitive type of social behavior, which can be called contactual behavior . . . and it is possible that higher types of social behavior had their origin in this simple adaptation."

Agonistic behavior. All organisms become involved at one time or another in a struggle with other organisms or with nature. Fighting or protective behavior is included under the term agonistic from the Greek root meaning "to struggle."

Sexual behavior. Almost all animals show sexual activity in one form or another, ranging from contact and courtship to coition.

Care-giving behavior. In higher animals once the young of a species are born there is usually a period of time during which they are comparatively helpless. During this time, nurturant or succorant behavior is provided by the adult members of the group. This is not necessarily parental behavior, since in some groups, such as the bees, care of the young is provided by the workers who are sterile females. McDougall considered the parental drive one of seven basic instincts.

Care-soliciting behavior. The young of many species show various kinds of behavior which may be interpreted as care-seeking. Young birds make cheeping sounds and hold their opened beaks in the air, and the young of most higher species engage in behavior which seems to elicit care-giving responses from the adult members of the group.

Eliminative behavior. Many animals have special patterns of behavior associated with the elimination of waste products. Many birds, for example, flip their tail at the moment the feces are released so the material is tossed away. Dogs and cats will dig holes and bury their excrement, and so on.

Allelomimetic behavior. This is defined as "behavior in which two or more animals do the same thing, with some degree of mutual stimulation." It is illustrated by the integrated flight of flocks of birds, by the migration of schools of fish, and by the grazing behavior of many herbivorous animals. It implies imitative behavior, although it is not clear to what extent such activity is learned.

Investigative behavior. This is often called exploratory behavior and may be thought of as a method animals use for getting to know the environment. What learning theorists usually call operant behavior would probably be included under this heading. McDougall elevated curiosity to the status of an instinct and defined it as an "impulse to approach and to examine more closely the object that excites it."

Several important points may be made in reviewing these nine types of adaptive behavior. Some of them do not fit the criteria listed earlier for basic emotions or basic adaptive processes. Care-giving and care-soliciting behavior are found only in higher animals and are thus not applicable to all levels of evolutionary development. Allelomimetic behavior is found only in certain groups of animals and requires, in any case, highly developed sense organs for distance reception. Shelter-seeking behavior may be thought of as learned behavior that the higher organisms show; at lower levels, it is hardly more than a tendency to keep moving until external conditions are not too dissimilar from internal ones. It is really not a pattern at all.

Of the nine adaptive processes listed by Scott, therefore, only five fit our criteria. Of these, agonistic behavior should be considered at greater length.

Scott classifies both flight and fight under the general heading of agonistic behavior. These tendencies, however, are so different and are expressed in such different ways that it is desirable to provide separate categories for them. In fight behavior the tendency is to destroy the opponent or to destroy the barrier to the satisfaction of some need. In flight behavior there is the need to avoid being destroyed; the organism shows either escape behavior, withdrawal, contraction, or freezing. It is thus suggested that Scott's agonistic behavior be broken down into destruction behavior and protection behavior.

Two other modifications of Scott's classification should be made. An organism may eliminate not only at the anal end but at the oral end as well. When some noxious material is ingested, the body usually reacts by ejecting this material, or "vomiting" it. At the human level, this is usually associated with the feeling of disgust. McDougall described this process as "repugnance" and considered it a basic impulse. He called it the "instinct of repulsion." He noted correctly that this is another kind of protection response of the organism.

A different basic pattern is the reaction to loss or deprivation. This may perhaps be illustrated by reference to some human parallels. A man in love may tell his sweetheart that she fills his heart; an attractive child may elicit the comment from an adult that he could eat her up. Both imply a kind of incorporation of desired objects. If the pleasureful object is, in some sense, lost, then there results a pattern of reaction usually thought of as sadness or grief and which may be described in the general case as a deprivation reaction. It is suggested that the essence of this prototype pattern is the ubiquitous fact of hunger and the organism's reactions to loss of food. Experiences of grief in human beings are often characterized in terms of feeling "empty," "lost," "alone," or as if there is a "gap" which cannot be filled. Only in recent years has some research been directed toward identifying the nature of this deprivation pattern in detail. Thus, to the list of behavior patterns Scott has presented, deprivation might be added.

There is one final addition to Scott's list of basic biological processes. Magda Arnold (1960) has marshaled cogent arguments for the view that most emotions involve an intuitive appraisal of a stimulus as good (beneficial) or bad (harmful). Now although evaluations of harm and benefit may be involved in emotions, it is very unlikely that all organisms can unequivocally evaluate all stimuli with which they make contact. Some period, extended or brief, is necessary before tissue damage occurs, or internal injury develops, or pleasurable sensations occur. During this initial period of direct contact with an unevaluated object, a pattern of behavior apparently develops which, at the human level, is usually called surprise. It is therefore suggested that a pattern of behavior called contact behavior or orientation be added to the original list.

It is thus possible to arrive at eight basic behavior patterns which may be found in some form at all levels of evolution, which do not depend on particular neural structures or body parts, which do not depend on introspections, and which are defined in terms of gross behavioral interactions between organism and environment. *It is suggested that these represent the basic dimensions of emotion applicable to all organismic levels. They represent the prototypes of all emotional behavior.*

The following list summarizes these basic prototypic* dimensions:

Incorporation. The act of taking in or ingesting food represents a basic prototypic pattern of behavior indicating *acceptance* of stimuli from the outside world into the organism. Such stimuli may be thought of as generally being beneficial or pleasurable for the individual.

Rejection. This represents a kind of riddance reaction. It is the prototype of behavior involved in getting rid of something harmful *which has already been incorporated.* It may take two forms, such as expelling feces or vomiting.

Destruction. This prototypic pattern of behavior occurs when the organism contacts a barrier to the satisfaction of some need, and consists essentially *in an attempt to*

---

* Prototype is defined as "an original or model after which anything is formed; the pattern of anything to be engraved, cast, etc.; exemplar; archetype."

destroy the barrier. If the barrier is another animal, it may be killed or it may even be eaten. At the lowest organismic levels the destruction of a barrier and the incorporation of food are fused into a single pattern which at higher levels is gradually differentiated. But only at the very highest levels, i.e., in man, is mass destruction carried out with no intention of incorporating the victims. And apparently only in man is the individual himself perceived as a barrier to the satisfaction of his own needs so that destruction is attempted in various ways against himself.

Protection. The prototypic protection response occurs basically under conditions of pain, although it may later occur under conditions of threats of pain or destruction. It is an attempt to avoid being destroyed. An organism in such a situation retreats, if possible. If flight is not possible, it makes itself as inconspicuous as it can by freezing, playing dead, or contracting to the smallest possible volume. (An analogy might be a group of soldiers pulling back into a small, tight circle to provide the best defense possible.) Although the description of this dimension might seem to imply consciousness on the part of an organism, this is not what is meant. The protection response to a stimulus is a basic protoplasmic reaction found in all organisms from the amoeba to man. Needless to say, in the life of most animals, protection responses are more necessary and meaningful (and perhaps even more frequent) than most other types, and thus they must play a central role in affecting all behavior.

Reproduction. This term is used to represent the prototypic response associated with sexual behavior. Apparently at almost all animal levels, sexual behavior is associated with some form of pulsatile or orgastic behavior. Even the asexual reproduction of one-celled organisms has an intense pulsating quality as recorded by high speed photography. Pleasure is presumably associated with all forms of sexual behavior, and may be defined in terms of approach and maintenance-of-contact tendencies.

Deprivation. The loss of a pleasureful object which has been contacted or incorporated is associated with a prototypic behavior pattern which, at the human level, is generally described as grief or sadness. The word deprivation is defined as the pattern of reaction to the loss of something possessed or enjoyed.

Orientation is the pattern of behavior which occurs when an organism contacts a new or strange object. This reaction is typically quite transient and exists so long as the object remains unevaluated in terms of harm or benefit, pain or pleasure. As soon as the object or stimulus is evaluated (without, necessarily, self-consciousness), this pattern of surprise changes to one (or more) of the other patterns. If the object produces pain, the pattern becomes protection; if it produces pleasure, the pattern may change to incorporation or reproduction.

Exploration. This refers to the more-or-less random activities organisms use to explore their environment. The form of these activities depends a great deal upon the type of sensory endowment of the organism, some animals utilizing their tactile sense much more than others. Paramecia alternate between going forward and back, while birds, who have excellent distance receptors, explore large portions of their environment at a glance. Exploratory activity seems to be spontaneous and almost continuous in most animals. It is prototypic of what humans call curiosity and play.

These then represent the eight prototypic dimensions of emotion: *incorporation, rejection, destruction, protection, reproduction, deprivation, orientation,* and *exploration.* These basic dimensions apply to all organismic levels from the lowest up to man. The terms used to describe them refer to overt behavior patterns or involve concepts like pleasure and pain which are definable in terms of overt behavior.

This latter point has been most effectively developed by Young (1952, 1959). He notes that affective processes (i.e., pleasures and pains) may be objectively defined by their attributes: a) approach-maintaining behavior refers to positive affect; avoidance-terminating behavior to negative affect; and b) affective processes vary in intensity along a bipolar axis. Young marshals considerable evidence to show that there is a difference between sensory intensity and affective intensity, and that the latter state can be measured by various food preference tests, as well as by the technique of self-stimulation of the brain. He concludes that "Neuro-behavioral patterns are organized according to the hedonic principle of maximizing the positive and minimizing the negative affective arousal." He also concludes that "it would be unfortunate if the fear of subjectivism served to obstruct a much-needed development of hedonic theory."

The problem that now arises is how to utilize these conceptions concerning primary emotions to develop an integrated theory that accounts for *all* emotions and that has implications for research. This task will be attempted in the remaining chapters.

6

The Evolution of
Primary Emotions: I

Ethology . . . does make an impressive contribution to the chorus of voices which are emphasizing the essential unity of living things and the similarity, in much that is fundamental, between animals and man.

—WILLIAM H. THORPE

Darwin was among the first to recognize that the concept of evolution which he had postulated should apply not only to the development of physical structures but to the evolution of mind and emotions as well. In *Expression of Emotion in Man and Animals*, which he published in 1872, he gave many illustrations of parallel ways emotions are expressed in different organisms. He felt that such observations would provide a safe basis for generalization on the causes or origin of various types of expressive behavior, since the expressions of animals, in contrast to men, are not likely to be conventional.

The expansion of research has confirmed Darwin's conception of the basic unity of the living system in its various manifestations. A biologist makes this evaluation:

> . . . it is the conclusion of many and various disciplines that the world of living things appears now as far more of a unity than was conceivable one hundred years ago. The post-Darwinian era in research has tended, on the whole, to break down barriers alike between phyla and between individual disciplines, and the same fundamental general principles are seen to be operating fairly widely through the animal and plant kingdom. Even the bacteria and the viruses, for all their strangeness, seem less remote than they once did (Thorpe, 1957).

There seems little question that basic processes exist in common at all levels of biologic development. At the same time, it must be recognized that evolution has introduced something new in the structure and behavior of living organisms. We are thus faced with a twofold problem: first, to recognize the basic common elements found at all evolutionary levels, and secondly, to recognize and identify the newly emergent characteristics which are also evident.

The first point was elaborated in the preceding chapter in terms of prototypic emotions common to all levels of development. This chapter discusses the metamorphoses that occur in the patterns of expression of the eight prototypes in the course of phylogenetic development. Since the evidence on this question is relatively sparse, some of the analysis must remain speculative. Hopefully, however, a restatement of the problem will direct the attention of investigators to the gaps in our knowledge which must be filled.

In the 1928 Wittenberg Symposium, Piéron pointed out that in the least differentiated organisms, such as the protozoa, responses to stimulation are relatively limited and tend to center around the two basic patterns of attraction to certain objects and avoidance of others. These responses, he concluded, "may be characterized as affective reactions of a primitive sort." Differentiated patterns of emotion occur only among the higher animals with well-developed nervous systems. "It is in the Hymenoptera, the Cephalopoda, and at least the higher Vertebrata (all of which have associative areas either in subesophageal nervous ganglia, or in the brain) that we find the characteristic expressions of emotion, which take the form of agitation, of cutaneous, cardio-vascular and visceral manifestations."

The idea of a few simple patterns in lower organisms centering around approach and withdrawal has been expressed by several authors. Turner (1957) reports that fish withdraw from high frequency sounds and approach low frequency sources. Scott (1958) notes that certain types of protozoa will swim away from strong sunlight but swim toward weak light. Schneirla (1959) has generalized this observation as a principle that "low intensities of stimulation tend to evoke approach responses, high intensity, withdrawal responses from the source." Reich (1949) has stated that emotion is an "expressive plasmatic motion, (that) pleasurable stimuli cause an emotion" (or "moving out") of the protoplasm from the center towards the periphery. Conversely, unpleasurable stimuli cause an emotion—or rather, remotion—from the periphery to the center of the organism. These two basic directions of biophysical plasma current correspond to the two basic affects of the psychic apparatus, pleasure and anxiety." One of the expressions of psychic disturbance in humans, according to Reich, is the development of muscle tensions in roughly concentric sequential rings around the body, which he interprets as indicating a basic metameric organization in man and which he calls "the worm in man."

These views concerning the patterns of approach and withdrawal, in the light of the present conception, seem unduly narrow. Although it is true that the lowest forms of life are greatly limited in the possibilities of action, yet it is unlikely that there are only two kinds of behavior available. As noted earlier, even an amoeba can show de-

structive action, protective behavior, exploratory behavior
and ejection of incorporated materials. However, the
amoeba can destroy only by incorporation of an object,
so that these two basic patterns are fused. Similarly there
is no distinction between rejection by vomiting and rejection by evacuation of waste materials. The possibilities of
withdrawal in an amoeba are limited to contraction or
gross movement of the entire body, whereas in higher
animals partial withdrawals of body parts may occur. Thus,
although we may identify the eight prototypic patterns in
the lowest organisms, they are less separate, less clear-cut,
and less involved with complex learning, than in higher
organisms.

Transition to Man

To the extent that there are basic patterns of emotion observable in all organisms, they must also be found in higher
animals and in man. But the problem this poses is: what
forms do the prototypic patterns take in man, how are
they recognized, and how are they named?

Turner (1957) draws some picturesque parallels, pointing out the

> fundamental similarity between two adult male Sia-
> mese fighting fish with their gill coverings spread out,
> circling one another, and the intimidation behavior of
> Tom Sawyer and Alfred Temple. This resemblance is
> more than superficial. The specific evocative signals
> differ: Tom Sawyer would not bristle at sight of
> *Betta splendens.* The total body response differs in
> many ways, yet there are underlying constancies in
> motor innervation . . . that convey a universal mean-
> ing, not only within, but also between vertebrate
> species.

The same point is made by Kempf (1953), who suggests that behavior may be described as "acquisitive,"
"avoidant," "assimilative," or "eliminative," and draws

parallels between these basic patterns and human activity. For example, he defines "assimilative" as "the taking into itself bodily of nutritional substances" and then says that this includes "the acceptance into its integrative self of the harmonious, pleasurable effects of internal and external stimulation, such as love of certain beautiful parts of the body or abilities and social approvals and praises, memories, beliefs, ideas, and external possessions (home, nest, parents, mate, children, friends, clothing, tools, books, icons, etc.)." He similarly uses the term "elimination" to refer to the ejection from the body of waste materials, as well as the rejection of memories of failures and mistakes, disapproval, and so on.

Scott's interesting book *Animal Behavior* (1958) describes many examples of complex social and emotional interactions in animals which are similar to those in man. For example, various forms of communication exist between animals. Most bird species have at least six or seven different calls which can easily be related to such things as hunger, warning, distress, food, and so on. Dogs have been found to have a limited period early in life during which affectional ties can be built up with humans. If contact is initiated later on, such ties are extremely difficult to establish. Fighting between members of the same species is rarely seen except in organisms capable of rapid movement. Such fighting occurs in arthropods, reptiles, birds, and almost all species of vertebrates, although its specific forms depend on such things as the presence of teeth, horns, claws, and vocalizing organs.

The continuing studies by Harlow (1958, 1959) of the effect of surrogate mothers on the behavior and development of monkeys has produced a wealth of interesting information. Apparently the infant monkeys preferred a surrogate mother made of terry cloth and foam rubber to one made of wire, implying some kind of contact satisfaction from the former. Most of these monkeys, however, have not developed normally. They have tended to remain isolated, withdrawn, asocial creatures who engage in little spontaneous play and although sexually mature, have not generally entered into sexual activity.

In general, evidence for emotional parallels in the behavior patterns of animals and men have been accumulating since the classic work of Darwin. Many authors have pointed out that the snarl of the dog is the sneer of the human being and that the same muscle in both cases uncovers the canine, our single vestige of a pointed tooth. Difficulties arise, however, in the problem of naming emotions in both animals and men, particularly since emotions exist in different degrees and different names are often used to represent them. The problem of naming, though, is not peculiar to either psychology or the study of emotions but exists in all sciences. The development of the concept of color is a good illustration. The word color has been used to refer to subjective experiences, to a property of dyes, pigments, and stains (or colorants), and to spectral characteristics of light. These various usages led to confusion until in 1952 a committee of the American Standards Association established, after careful analysis, a series of unequivocal definitions that could be consistently applied to these various areas.

McDougall (1921) also noted that the adaptation of a word from common speech to scientific usage usually indicates a change of meaning. With special reference to the naming of emotions, William James wrote: "The internal shadings of emotional feeling, moreover, merge endlessly into each other. Language has discriminated some of them, as hatred, antipathy, animosity, dislike, aversion, malice, spite . . . etc., but in the dictionaries of synonyms we find these feelings distinguished more by their severally appropriate objective stimuli than by their conscious or subjective tone." It is thus reasonable to expect that the process of naming the prototypic patterns when found at different levels will not always be easy or evident. A criterion that must be followed, however, is that the theory which is eventually developed be internally consistent and be capable of stimulating research.

Expression of Prototypic Patterns
in Higher Animals

It is generally evident with what emotions in man most of
the prototypic patterns may be identified. The destruction
pattern would be associated with anger, the protection
pattern with fear, the rejection pattern with disgust, the
deprivation pattern with sorrow, the reproduction pattern
with joy, and the incorporation pattern with acceptance.
The orientation pattern would be most closely related to
startle and the exploration pattern with something like
curiosity or expectation.

Each of these emotions implies an *intensity dimension*
as well, so that apprehension and terror are both associated
with the protection pattern. Similarly annoyance and rage
may both be associated with the destruction pattern.
In the discussion in this chapter of fear, anger, disgust,
etc., it should be recognized that these terms are used as
shorthand expressions for groups of emotion words which
sample an intensity dimension at different points.

Before proceeding to a description of the organization
and interaction of these primary emotions, it would help
to have a clear description of their properties. Ideally
these emotions should be produced in lower animals and
in man and their characteristics measured and described.
Unfortunately this has rarely been done, and because of
the problem of purity is very difficult to do. We must rely
for the most part on descriptions provided by careful observers, biologists and psychologists, who have reported
their findings on the basis of field studies, clinic observations, or laboratory studies. Without attempting to be
exhaustive, the following sections will present some of
these observations on primary emotions in higher animals
and in man. Some duplication will be evident, but this
should illustrate the consistencies in the forms of expressions of the primary emotions.

The Fear Dimension

We shall begin our survey with a description of the fear dimension. Fear has occupied a prominent place in most discussions of emotions;° it has even been described as the "central problem of neurosis" (Freud, 1936). Its importance is probably related to the fact that "since stressing and potentially destructive conditions far outnumber and outweigh the constructive conditions, readiness for avoidance reaction generally dominates readiness for acquisitive action" (Kempf, 1958). Shakespeare said, "Of all the bad passions fear is most accursed."

Darwin gave many detailed descriptions of fear in higher animals and in man. The following is quoted from his classic work:

> With all or almost all animals, even with birds, terror causes the body to tremble. The skin becomes pale, sweat breaks out, and the hair bristles. The secretions of the alimentary canal and of the kidneys are increased, and they are involuntarily voided, owing to the relaxation of the sphincter muscles, as is known to be the case with man, and as I have seen with cattle, dogs, cats, and monkeys. The breathing is hurried. The heart beats quickly, wildly, and violently; but whether it pumps the blood more efficiently through the body may be doubted, for the surface seems bloodless and the strength of the muscles soon fails. . . . The mental faculties are much disturbed. Utter prostration soon follows, and even fainting. . . . Birds when frightened, as a general rule, closely depress all their feathers, and their consequently diminished size is often astonishing. . . . Mr. Sutton has distinctly seen the face of the Macacus rhesus grow pale from fear. Monkeys also tremble from fear; and sometimes they void their excretions. . . . Abject fear is exhibited by the relaxation of all muscles,

° No attempt will be made at this point to distinguish between fear and anxiety or any of the other synonyms that are sometimes used interchangeably.

the head seems to sink between the shoulders. . . . Fear is often preceded by astonishment. In both cases the eyes and mouth are widely opened, and the eyebrows raised. The frightened man at first stands like a statue motionless and breathless, or crouches down as if instinctively to escape observation. . . . This paleness of the (skin) surface, however, is probably in large part, or exclusively, due to the vasomotor center being affected in such a manner as to cause the contraction of the small arteries of the skin. . . . Perspiration immediately exudes from it. This exudation is all the more remarkable, as the surface is then cold, and hence the term a cold sweat; whereas, the sudorific glands are properly excited into action when the surface is heated. The hairs also on the skin stand erect, and the superficial muscles shiver. In connection with the disturbed action of the heart, the breathing is hurried. The salivary glands act imperfectly; the mouth becomes dry, and is often opened and shut. I have also noticed that under slight fear there is a strong tendency to yawn. One of the best-marked symptoms is the trembling of all the muscles of the body; and this is often first seen in the lips. As fear increases into an agony of terror . . . there is a gasping and convulsive motion of the lips, a tremor on the hollow cheek, a gulping and catching of the throat—the uncovered and protruding eyeballs are fixed on the object of terror, or they may roll restlessly from side to side. The pupils are said to be enormously dilated. All the muscles of the body may become rigid, or may be thrown into convulsive movements. . . .

This passage was quoted at such length because most observers who have since written on this topic have either repeated or supplemented some aspect of it.

In *The Principles of Psychology*, William James makes an important point about fear which is consistent with Darwin's description but at variance with Cannon's later analysis of fear as a flight pattern. He writes that "the trembling and the palsy [in fear] make [the animal] incapable of flight or defence; . . . in the most decisive moments of danger we are less able to see (or to think) than when we are tranquil. In the face of such facts we must admit that the phenomena of fear cannot all be accounted for by selection. Their extreme degrees are morbid phenomena which show an imperfection in the organism."

In the 1928 Wittenberg Symposium, Piéron makes essentially the same point, citing examples of birds and even kittens who died as a result of fear connected with handling and without any direct injury. He concludes that although some of the bodily changes during fear may be useful, most are indifferent and some are harmful.

This observation of the enervating character of high intensity fear made by Darwin, James, and Piéron but ignored by many other writers has been documented by Arnold (1960, vol. 2). She cites studies which indicate that rats and dogs show a reduction of activity under conditions designed to produce either acute or chronic fear. In humans, patients with acute anxiety are reported able to work on an exhausting treadmill only half as long as normal subjects. Patients with chronic anxiety work only half as well as the patients with acute anxiety.

The pharmacological evidence collected thus far seems to indicate that the adrenalin secreted during fear reduces muscular performance by "increasing lactic acid formation and by interfering with glucose and oxygen utilization." It is quite possible, however, that low levels of fear (i.e., mild apprehension) may actually improve performance, since Burn (1945) has shown that adrenalin in weak concentrations improves cholinergic transmission but depresses it in high concentrations. This suggests that a low level of fear results in optimum muscular efficiency.

Some other writers on the physiology of fear have noted that the contraction of the peripheral blood vessels does act as a protective device since it prevents an excess flow of blood from wounds received during any fight or attack (Bekhterev, 1928). Kempf (1953) has reported that in conditions of fear, when an organism is unable to escape from a source of danger or pain, the pulse becomes very rapid and small and is accompanied by an increase in blood pressure, while under conditions of intense panic, with an extremely rapid pulse, the blood pressure will drop and will be associated with general weakness, trembling, or even fainting. Claparède (1928) claims that such symptoms of fear will only occur in an individual if he cannot escape from the pain or danger. McDougall (1921) has described fear as the "great inhibitor of action . . . and becomes in primitive human societies the great agent of social discipline." It is thus evident that many observers, from Darwin to the present day, have found high intensity fear essentially incapacitating and not capable of facilitating flight.

These observations suggest that high intensity fear may be adaptive only in the limited sense of protectively modifying peripheral circulation in the face of imminent destruction. At lower intensities, fear is an adaptive flight-from-danger pattern.

The Opposition of Fear and Anger

There are several descriptions of the essentially opposite character of fear and anger:

—"The fear-impulse [is] the most opposed in tendency to the pugnacious" (McDougall, 1921).
—"[Fear] operates by leading away from, [and anger] by leading towards and destroying" (Tolman, 1923).
—"The overt response in fear we may call avoidance, and in anger attack" (Woodworth, 1928).
—"Anger is correlated with an aggressive attack against obstacles, while fear is associated with the opposite type of behavior" (Carr, 1929).
—"Anger is differentiated from fear chiefly in that it is an active attack on a situation rather than a retreat from it" (Valentine, 1941).

Woodworth makes another important point in the paper cited above. The identification of avoidance or attack behavior cannot be made in terms of isolated movements of parts of the body since any one action may mean different things. A man who draws his hand back may have just been burned, or he may be getting ready to strike a blow. Avoidance or attack must be definable, he suggests, in terms of the total body action of trying to get away from something or destroying it.

OTHER SIGNS OF FEAR

There are, however, some isolated expressions, at least in higher animals, which are very frequently, if not invariably, associated with fear. In a questionnaire study of how parents identify fear in their children, the following were usually mentioned: crying, screaming; running away, withdrawing, retreating, dodging, shrinking; clinging to adults, clutching, reaching for help; startle, "jerks"; and certain facial expressions, such as eyes wide, face pale and downcast, etc. (Valentine, 1941).

There are numerous literary and proverbial descriptions of fear, many of which are echoed in Darwin. Some of the more graphic are: "fear has big eyes" and "trembling like a leaf" (proverbial); and "Pale fear seized everyone" (Homer), "Fear runs away with my tongue" (Aeschylus), "You make my hair stand on end and my flesh creep" (Dickens), "A cold sweat bedewed all my limbs" (Vergil), "Pale as his shirt, his knees knocking each other" (Shakespeare), "Like an aspen leaf he quaked" (Chaucer).

Here are some common expressions used in connection with fear: cold feet, cold sweat, shaking in his boots, scared stiff, rooted (or frozen) to the spot, petrified, cold with fear, hair stood on end, knees were knocking, blood turned to ice, butterflies in his stomach, white with fear, teeth chattering.

To all of these expressions and proverbs should be added the results of Klineberg's study (1938) on the description of emotional expression in Chinese literature. By examining various Chinese novels and books, Klineberg shows that the alleged inscrutability of the Chinese is greatly exaggerated, although there are various rules and recommendations which suggest modifications in the "natural" ways of expressing emotion, particularly grief. Fear is described in almost identical terms as in Western literature, e.g., "everyone trembled with a face the color of clay," "every one of his hairs stood on end, and the pimples came out on the skin all over his body," "a cold sweat broke forth on his whole body, and he trembled without ceasing," and "they were so frightened that their waters and wastes burst out of them." (Klineberg found similar parallels for anger, sorrow, and shame.) *

In summary, all of these quotations and descriptions from widely varying literary sources and from common experience imply considerable consistency in the forms of expression of emotion, particularly of fear.

A further comment which should be made at this point concerns the difference between fear and anxiety. In Freud's last major discussion of the problem of anxiety (1936), he concluded:

> It is an important advance in self-protection when this traumatic situation of helplessness (discomfort) is not merely awaited but is foreseen, anticipated . . . Anxiety is the expectation of the trauma on the one hand, and on the other, an attenuated repetition of it. . . . Anxiety is undeniably related to expectation; one feels anxious lest something occur.

This obviously implies that anxiety is a learned response, but learned on what basis?

Mowrer (1939) concludes that anxiety is "the conditioned form of the pain reaction." Sullivan (1956) clarifies the distinction between fear and anxiety in the following way. Fear, according to him, is a generally found, self-protective reaction to a painful or novel situation; anxiety,

* There are also some expressions which are not the same; for example, "They stretched out their tongues" indicates surprise, and "He clapped his hands" indicates disappointment. These may be thought of as conventional expressions. An interesting description of hatred is "He would fain have swallowed him at a gulp" which obviously implies destruction through eating.

on the other hand, is a product of education. To restate his argument, fear is an unconditioned (unlearned) response to a potentially destructive stimulus (usually direct pain), while anxiety is a conditioned fear response to a new situation. This is illustrated by the fact (Valentine, 1941) that the fears observed in infants are related to transient but specific stimuli (e.g., loud noise, dropping, strange people, etc.); but as the child grows older, the fears are replaced by anxieties of an anticipatory or imaginary character (darkness, ghosts, being "bad," etc.).

We have thus established a reasonably consistent picture of the characteristics associated with the dimension of fear. The following chapter will discuss the interrelations of fear with other emotions.

The Dimension of Anger

The emotion of anger, with its various synonyms and derivatives has probably been discussed more extensively in the literature than any other emotion, with the possible exception of fear. Many of the methods of social control, for adults and children, are concerned with the socializing of the tendency to react with anger to various situations. Psychoanalytic theory utilizes a variety of terms which involve anger in some form, for instance, sadism, aggression, death instinct, resentment, hate, hostility, and so on. In the theorizing on emotion, academic psychologists have generally used anger and fear as a basis for analysis, as if these emotions were typical of all the rest.

What are the properties and characteristics of anger that make it so central in discussions of emotion? In the next few pages, some of the literature on anger and aggression will be reviewed for a tentative answer to this question.

Freud (1922) has raised the possibility that aggression is the oldest impulse of all and is probably present in the unicellular amoeba. In a review of the literature on aggression, Jackson, a psychoanalyst, writes (1954) that "its source appears to be the emotion of anger, and its aim the destruction of the object which arouses this emotion.

. . . Aggression is, primarily, an expression of vitality (and) is a *sine qua non* of individual survival." In a similar vein, Reich (1942) writes: "A living being develops a *destructive* impulse when it wants to destroy a source of danger. . . . *We destroy in a danger situation because we want to live and because we do not want to suffer anxiety*." Reich also comments that although the aim of destruction is not pleasure, yet the release from the painful (or frustrating) situation producing the anger is a pleasurable experience. From this point of view it is possible to think of anger when expressed successfully as a pleasurable tension release. This point is of some importance and will be discussed later. Sullivan (1956) points out that "anger is one of the ways of handling anxiety that we learn early . . . Its purpose presumably is not to enable us to escape threatening or injurious situations, but to destroy them or drive them away."

These definitions by analytically-oriented writers are consistent with the definitions proposed by other researchers in the field. Sears, Hovland, and Miller (1940) in their studies of aggression define it as "an impulse to destroy, damage, torment, retaliate, blow up, humiliate, insult, threaten or intimidate." In Goodenough's study of anger in young children (1931), she says that anger usually takes "the form of some sort of motor or verbal attack upon the offender," although it sometimes has the appearance of an explosive form of outlet. Valentine (1941) points out that anger responses occur when an individual is somehow blocked in the activity he is engaged in or about to become engaged in, and is identified by such acts as kicking, stamping, striking, screaming, etc. In a factor-analytic study of anger ratings assigned to various types of situations, Iverson (1955) concludes that "anger is most likely to occur in connection with descriptions of situations which contain insurmountable barriers to the reaching of goals, and least likely to arise in connection with references to sensory or physiological stimulation." These definitions are more or less typical of those usually used.

Another point of interest is the question of how anger

is expressed in lower organisms. Scott (1958), for example, reports that by the time a mouse is twelve days of age, it will bite anything that injures it and by the age of one month will attack a strange mouse. At still lower levels, in fish (e.g., cichlids), it has been observed that a newcomer introduced into an already occupied tank will cause the possessor to erect his median fins, intensify his color and move toward the intruder. If this does not produce retreat, the fish circle one another, sometimes with tail beating, butting, or nipping and occasionally with mouth-mouth biting or eye enucleation. Quite typically, when one fish is attacked by others, the scales are eaten off (Turner, 1957).

Higher animals show clear-cut anger reactions which Darwin has described in detail. He writes: "Mr. Sutton has often observed the face of the Macacus rhesus, when much enraged, growing red. . . . When the Mandrill is in any way excited, the brilliantly colored, naked parts of the skin are said to become still more vividly colored." At a later point in his book, Darwin describes the signs of anger in men.

The face reddens or becomes purple, the veins on the forehead and neck are distended. The reddening of the skin has been observed with the copper-colored Indians of South America, and even as it is said, on the white cicatrices left by old wounds on negroes. . . . The eyes are always bright. . . . They are sometimes bloodshot, and are said to protrude from their sockets—the result of the head being gorged with blood, as shown by the veins being distended. The pupils are always contracted in rage. The lips are commonly retracted, the grinning or clenched teeth being exposed. This retraction of the lips and uncovering of the teeth during paroxysms of rage, as if to bite the offender, is so remarkable, considering how seldom the teeth are used by men in fighting. The upper lip may be seen to be raised, especially at the corners, so that the huge canine teeth are exhibited.

This picture of anger presented by Darwin is elaborated still further by Cannon in two of his publications (1928, 1929). He writes:

> The rage response (crouching body, frowning brow, firm lips, clenched or grinding teeth, growled threats, tightened fists, etc.) is a complex attitude which we do not have to learn—its occurrence is a part of our native inheritance. It is a constant and uniform type of behavior, having features in common in widely scattered races of men and even in lower animals so that the nature of the attitude is at once understood without the necessity for words. It is a permanent mode of reaction; whether in childhood or old age, it differs only in minor details . . . Any hampering or checking of activity, or opposition to one or another primary impulse brings it out . . . These are the properties of a simple reflex, such as sneezing or coughing. (1929)

In the earlier paper Cannon had described anger in the following way:

> The complex of bodily alterations that appears in rage has many features resembling the simple reflexes, such as sneezing, coughing, and sucking. First, its occurrence in the early months of even so highly developed an organism as the human infant indicates that its neural pattern, like that of the reflexes mentioned above, is congenitally inwrought in the central nervous apparatus. Second, as in the reflexes, it is a prompt response to an appropriate stimulus. Again, it is a constant and uniform response—so much is this so, indeed, that there is no mistaking its character, whether it be manifested by the diverse races of man or by the lower animals. It is like the reflexes, also, in being a permanent mode of reaction; throughout life the characteristic display of the rage-response may be suddenly evoked in all its elaborateness. Further, it is a response to a fairly definite stimulus—an inner

stimulus which arises when there is a hampering or checking of motion or an opposition to one or another primary impulse. Finally, the rage-response is like the simple reflexes in being useful.

Cannon also notes that typical rage reactions can be made to appear even in animals deprived of the cerebral cortex. McDougall (1921) also had written that anger is produced when one or another of the instincts is obstructed in its free exercise.

More recent studies of physiological changes associated with anger have been summarized by Arnold (1960, vol. 2). She cites evidence showing that defecation may occur during intense fear but not anger, and that tears which may flow abundantly during temper tantrums are inhibited during fear. Anger appears to be associated with nor-adrenalin secretion with rise in blood pressure and with cholinergic vasodilatation. As mentioned in an earlier chapter, animals which prey upon others and attack and fight a good deal generally show a preponderance of nor-adrenalin in their adrenal medulla, while more timid animals show a relatively greater adrenalin secretion. Arnold concludes that a whole group of stressors such as heat, anger, mecholyl, and insulin have the common effect of producing cholinergic-type reactions with effects opposite to those of the adrenergic stressors. The paper by Kempf (1953) reports that in rage the heart develops slower, stronger, and larger contractions than in fear, thus sustaining a greater volume of blood at high pressure in order to support the somatic compulsion to destroy the cause of the anger.

Several questionnaire studies concerned with the expression of anger in humans have been done in the past, starting with Hall's report in 1899 (cited by Goodenough, 1931). Of over two thousand replies, 87 percent reported flushing of the face as characteristic of anger. Various other symptoms were stated as being associated with anger, for example: body tension; biting, grinding, or showing of the teeth; quivering or compressed lips; butting with the head in children; scratching, kicking, striking or throwing. The cry of anger is loud, sharp, and generally sustained, although some people reported snarling, growling, or grunting. In general, anger was associated with "a rather primitive impulse toward direct aggression." One additional symptom worth noting especially is that some people (both male and female) reported excitement of the sex organs during anger. This suggestion that anger and sex may have much in common is well-documented in the clinical literature on sadism.

In the study by Goodenough (1931), forty-five children (ages 7 months to 7 years) were observed by their parents over a period of about one month and a standard diary kept. One of the important findings was the transient nature of anger outbursts; in 3 cases out of 4, the outburst lasted less than four minutes, and in 1 case in 4, less than one minute. The duration of outbursts was unrelated to sex and changed very little during the first seven years of life. Another interesting observation is the fact that the number of outbursts increased when children were sick, constipated, hungry, or being trained for night bladder control, thus suggesting again that frustrations of any type produce anger.

Consistent with the earlier report by Watson, restriction of movement did increase anger outbursts, but this factor had less and less effect with older children. Goodenough concludes by saying "that with advancing age, the forms of behavior displayed during anger become more definitely directed toward a given end, while the primitive bodily responses of the infant and young child are gradually replaced by substitute reactions commonly of a somewhat less violent and more symbolic character."

Compare these reports on the nature of anger with some colloquial descriptions of anger. A person who is angry is commonly described as: hot under the collar, in a sweat, purple (livid) with rage, red, seeing red, gnashing his teeth, steaming, bristling with rage, fighting mad, hopping mad, breathing fire. These expressions imply a change of surface temperature and color, as well as a change of body movements.

The transient nature of anger is proverbial: "Delay is the antidote of anger"; "Nothing is benefited by delay except anger"; "When angry count ten before you speak. If very angry a hundred"; "Anger is a short madness."

Proverbs also emphasize the lack of rationality and sensory awareness during anger: "A man is a stark fool all the while he is angry"; "An angry man cannot see right"; "An angry man heeds no counsel"; "An angry man opens his mouth and shuts his eyes"; "When a man grows angry his reason rides out." An Italian proverb suggests a connection between anger and sex: "Anger increases love."

Various sources have thus presented a reasonably consistent picture of the nature of anger in animals and men. It appears as a reaction to obstacles of any kind, is usually quite transient, and is related in some way to the emotions of joy, love, and sex. The specific nature of this connection will be examined in the next chapter.

7 ⊑

The Evolution of
Primary Emotions: II

Affects are typical responses to typical demands, responses handed down from one generation to another in the form of potentialities.

—KARL LANDAUER

The Dimension of Joy

The prototypic dimension called reproduction is most closely related at the human level to the emotions of joy, love, or sex. Before summarizing some of the literature on these emotions, it will be important to describe observations leading to the conclusion that a close relation exists between joy and anger.

In 1807, Harry Siddons translated and revised a manual for actors which had originally been published on the continent of Europe. In this manual, he described the way in which different emotions may be expressed, and on anger and joy, he wrote the following:

Anger is indicated by the increased activity of the arms and hands, the inflamed and rolling eye, the grinding of teeth, the swelling of the veins of the face, neck and temples, a heavy and impetuous step, and an increased speed of all body movements. Increased speed of movement is also characteristic of joy; therefore the transition from anger to joy or vice versa can be made readily or abruptly, while the transition from anger to grief (or the reverse) needs to be done only by stages to be convincing.

This same idea was voiced by the British philosopher Spencer in 1890:

There are the dancings of joy as well as the stampings of anger . . . Anger shouts as well as joy; and often the noises made by children at play leave parents in doubt whether pleasure or pain is the cause. (Cited by Goodenough, 1931.)

Likewise according to classical psychoanalytic theory, since libidinal and death instincts are usually fused, one restraining the other, love and aggression will often occur in close association. Joan Riviere writes that "Both the self-preservative and love instincts *need a certain amount of aggression* if they are to attain satisfaction, that is, an aggressive element is an essential part of both these instincts in actual functioning" (cited in Jackson, 1954). Another way of looking at this is simply to recognize that both anger and joy (or love) are approach emotions, even though the specific effect of the approach is different. Darwin described both anger and joy as "exciting" emotions.

This idea of the similarity of anger and joy is consistent with a factor-analytic study of emotional traits performed by Cyril Burt (reported by Jackson, 1954). Burt found a bipolar grouping of emotions on an axis which he labeled aggression versus inhibition. Those subjects who were more easily aroused to joy were also more sociable, self-assertive, prone to anger and curiosity, and more attracted by the opposite sex. Those subjects in whom sorrow was more easily aroused were also more likely to experience fear, disgust, or submission. Both joy and aggression were used in the sense of outgoingness and expansiveness. In the light of these experiments, it seems reasonable to consider anger and joy as closely related, more so than, for example, anger and fear or anger and grief.

What other characteristics can be identified with the dimension of joy? In extensive speculation about this, Reich (1942) suggested that "sexuality could be nothing else than *the biological function of expansion* (out of the self) *from center to periphery.* Conversely, *anxiety* could be nothing but the reverse direction from *periphery to center* (back into the self)." The process of expansion and contraction of part or all of the body on the basis of mechanical tension, electrical charge and discharge, and mechanical relaxation, he refers to as a basic function of all living organisms, a function which is expressed in specific ways in cardiac action, intestinal activity, and orgastic behavior. Many pleasureful activities such as sucking, evacuating and copulating have a pulsatory character. Pulsation is a result of the continuous process of balancing internal pressures for discharge against an external membrane surface, resulting in alternating expansion and contraction. He illustrates this idea by a description of the functional antithesis of action between the sympathetic and parasympathetic system. Table 1 is based upon his discussion.

Reich concludes that, in general, the parasympathetic system is dominant whenever there is expansion, elongation, hyperemia, turgor, and pleasure and that the sympathetic dominates whenever the organism contracts and withdraws blood from the periphery.

Some of these ideas, which are admittedly speculative, do find support from more recent researches. For example, Mittlemann and Wolff (1943) studied skin temperature changes in patients during analytic sessions, and found that skin temperature increased when the patients ex-

TABLE 1

*The Opposite Action of the Sympathetic
and Parasympathetic Systems.*

	SYMPATHETIC SYSTEM	PARASYMPATHETIC SYSTEM
Chemical Factors	Calcium (group) Adrenalin Cholesterin H-ions	Potassium (group) Cholin Lecithin OH-ions
General Effect on Tissues	Decreased surface tension Dehydration Striated muscle: paralyzed or spastic Decreased electrical irritability Increased O_2-consumption Increased blood pressure	Increased surface tension Hydration (tumescence of tissues) Muscle: increased tonicity Increased electrical irritability Decreased O_2-consumption Decreased blood pressure
Central Vascular Effect	Systolic Heart muscle stimulated	Diastolic Heart muscle relaxed
Peripheral Vascular Effect	Vasoconstriction	Vasodilatation

pressed sexual feelings and pleasure, but decreased during verbal expressions of shame, guilt and anxiety. This implies an increased peripheral blood flow during states of pleasure and a decreased flow during anxiety.

In the Kinsey report (1948), a description of erotic arousal, based on 12,000 interviews, is given. There is an increase in peripheral circulation and a rise in surface temperature;

> a flow of blood into such distensible organs as the eyes, the lips, the lobes of the ears, the nipples of the breast, the penis of the male, and the clitoris, the genital labia and the vaginal walls of the female; a partial but often considerable loss of perceptive capacity (sight, hearing, touch, taste, smell); an increase in so-called nervous tension, some degree of rigidity of some part or of the whole of the body at the moment of maximum tension; and then a sudden release which produces local spasms or more extensive all-consuming convulsions.

Kinsey points out that erection of the penis has been observed immediately after birth and is almost a daily occurrence in infants and young children. The evidence indicates that sexual arousal may be produced by a wide variety of stimuli, particularly in children. For example, sexual reactions have been reported during such diverse situations as urinating, swimming, fast car riding, being punished, being near accidents, feeling anger, playing a musical solo, finding money, being yelled at, nocturnal dreams, etc. However by the late teens most males respond only to direct genital stimulation or specifically sexual symbols.

Kinsey also noted that orgasm has been observed in infants from at least the age of four months. Such orgastic behavior in infants is (with the exception of ejaculation in males) almost identical to that reported by adults.

> The behavior involves a series of gradual physiological changes, the development of rhythmic body movements with distinct penis throbs and pelvic thrusts, an obvious change in sensory capacities, a final tension of muscles, especially of the abdomen, hips and back, a sudden release with convulsions, including rhythmic anal contractions—followed by the disappearance of all symptoms.

These observations indicate that the function of pulsation, presumably associated with joy or pleasure and eventually with reproduction, is a basic biological prototypic reaction observable in infants as well as adults and also in lower animals.

In the psychological literature, although not a great deal is said about joy per se the comments are fairly consistent. Watson (1924) says that the emotion of "love" is produced by stroking and touching of erogenous zones and by rocking. Tolman (1923) points out that the responses involved all seem appropriate for further continuation of the stimulus. Carr (1929) writes that "joy is awakened by the sudden and unexpected attainment of a highly desired end." Banham (1950), in an experimental study of the development of affectionate behavior in infancy, notes that it tends to prolong, repeat, or enhance an agreeable situation.

One difficulty in summarizing the literature is that the emotion of joy is sometimes used more or less interchangeably with love.

Although love undoubtedly has an element of joy in it, the very many discussions of love from the point of view of psychology, philosophy, literature, sociology, and biology would suggest that it is a more complex, subtle emotion than joy. Just as it is necessary to distinguish anxiety from fear and aggression from anger, it is necessary to distinguish love from joy.

One of the most important and obvious distinctions is that joy is a transient emotion and love is a long-lasting state. In the study of hypnotically induced emotions referred to earlier (Bull and Gidro-Frank), the emotion of joy was always reported as very transient whenever it appeared. On the other hand, no one would take very seriously the claim that an individual had fallen in love for a few minutes or a few hours. Secondly love is perceived as being of greater complexity than joy and thus, by implication, as being composed of simpler units. It is easy to conceive of joy without love, but not of love without joy. From this point of view, joy may be thought of as a component of love, but only one of several. The systematic import of this distinction between love and joy will be made clear in the next chapter. Unfortunately there is a remarkably small amount of scientific material available about either.

The Dimension of Grief

The effects of deprivation or loss are seen quite commonly and have been described in the psychiatric literature in great detail. In their more persistent and morbid forms, they are referred to as melancholia or depressive psychosis; in their more normal expressions, they are referred to simply as sadness or grief.

In an historical approach, we should first examine Darwin's description of grief. He wrote:

> Persons suffering from excessive grief often seek relief by violent and almost frantic movements; but when their suffering is somewhat mitigated, yet *prolonged,* they no longer wish for action, but remain motionless and passive, or may occasionally rock themselves to and fro. The circulation becomes languid; the face pale; the muscles flaccid; the eyelids droop; the head hangs on the contracted chest; the lips, cheeks and lower jaw all sink downwards from their own weight. Hence all the features are lengthened; and the face of a person who hears bad news is said to fall. . . . The corners of the mouth are drawn downwards, which is so universally recognized as a sign of being out of spirits, that it is almost proverbial. . . . the breathing becomes slow and feeble, and is often interrupted by deep sighs. . . . the sighs of a sorrowful person, owing to his slow respiration and languid circulation, are eminently characteristic.

In *The Principles of Psychology* William James quotes Lange describing grief in essentially the same way:

The chief feature in the physiognomy of grief is perhaps its paralyzing effect on the voluntary movements. This effect is by no means as extreme as that which fright produces . . . It is a feeling of weariness . . . But . . . the vascular muscles are more strongly contracted than usual, so that the tissues and organs of the body become anaemic. The immediate consequence of this bloodlessness is pallor and shrunkenness . . . Another regular consequence of the bloodlessness of the skin is a feeling of cold and shivering. A constant symptom of grief is sensitiveness to cold, and difficulty in keeping warm. In grief, the inner organs are unquestionably anaemic as well as the skin.

Recent psychosomatic research has verified this prediction of Lange's concerning the effect of grief on inner organs. The studies cited earlier concerning the effect of different emotions on stomach and colonic activity is entirely consistent with this idea. Grief produces anaemia of inner surfaces as well as outer.

Another important observation made about grief is its opposite nature to joy or love. Darwin wrote that sorrow and joy show opposing characteristics. "The whole expression of a man in good spirits is exactly the opposite of that of one suffering from sorrow. In all the exhilarating emotions the eyebrows, eyelids, the nostrils, and the angles of the mouth are raised. In the depressing passions, it is the reverse. . . . In joy the face expands, in grief, it lengthens."

This idea of the opposite character of grief and joy has been expressed in many ways. In proverbs, for example, we are told that "Joy surfeited turns to sorrow," "Joy and sorrow usually succeed each other," "Sorrow is but the shadow of joy; joy is but the cloak of sorrow."

In the psychological literature, we find such comments as the following: "Grief we look upon as being a reactive state (connected with love, really) in which the object or situation which usually calls out in the subject the reactions of love is suddenly removed" (Watson, 1921), or "Grief and sorrow are usually awakened by the loss of highly desirable conditions. . . . Joy is awakened by the sudden and unexpected attainment of a highly desired end" (Carr, 1928). Sullivan (1956) writes: "Grief in this biologically human sense is dependent on the integrative tendency which I call love—the capacity for intimacy."

Perhaps the most extensive and detailed discussions of grief and sorrow are found in the psychoanalytic literature, although here, too, not enough research has been done. Bowlby (1960), for example, suggests that "despite the early work of Freud and Abraham and the constant insistence of Melanie Klein, the significance for psychopathology of grief and mourning, especially when they occur in infancy and early childhood, has been and still is too little recognized." However, in the past few years some interesting observations have been made on young children who have suffered deprivation or loss of parents.

For example, Spitz and Wolf (1946) observed a group of children who had had good relations with their mothers for the first six months of life and then (for some reason) lost contact for at least three months. Under these conditions, the infants began to cry a good deal and began to show an increasing lack of response to contact by other people. These infants developed a dejected expression on their faces, slow movement and even stupor, insomnia, decreased appetite and weight loss, and eventually retarded development. Since these reactions occurred so early in infancy, it suggests that the response to loss of a pleasurable stimulus or object is a prototypic pattern, even though it may be modified by later experience. In this connection, Suttie (1952) has suggested that a fear of loneliness or loss is the conscious expression in adults of the drive for self-preservation which originally attached the infant to its mother. And Spitz (1957) has noted that infants and children in situations of deprivation or loss tend to regress to patterns of behavior which are ontogenetically earlier, for example, "negative cephalogyric motion," or "head-turning" behavior.

Among the most extensive observations on grief in childhood is the work of Bowlby (1960). He describes three
phases in the sequence of responses young children show
when they are removed from their mothers and placed
with strangers; he calls them protest, despair, and detachment and he believes they do not differ in any essential
aspect from those responses observed in adults on loss of
a loved object.

If a child over the age of six months is removed from
his mother,

> he will often cry loudly, shake his cot, throw himself
> about, and look eagerly towards any sight or sound
> which might prove to be his missing mother. This, the
> phase of Protest, may with ups and downs continue
> for as long as a week or more. . . . Sooner or later,
> however, despair sets in. . . . Ultimately, the rest-
> less noisy demands cease; he becomes apathetic and
> withdrawn, a despair broken only perhaps by an in-
> termittent and monotonous wail.

Finally in the stage of detachment, the child acts as if he
ceased to care.

The symptoms of separation and loss may be grouped
under three general categories, according to Anna Freud
(1960): a) psychosomatic symptoms—sleeping disturb-
ances, feeding troubles, digestive upsets, especially constipation, an increased susceptibility to sore throats, etc.;
b) regression in instinct development—clinging, domineer-
ing and greedy behavior, thumb sucking, rocking, biting,
spitting, hitting, etc.; and c) regression in ego development—changes of speech and loss of bowel and bladder
control.

In several studies of weaning in other cultures (cited
by Bowlby), it has been reported that temper tantrums
and other signs of hostility are frequently observed, although in our own culture this seems to depend upon how
gradual the weaning process is. Bowlby concludes that
"we are still singularly ignorant of the effects on infants
and young children of weaning per se. . . . Infantile de-

pendence (is) more than oral dependence, and instead of being confined to the first year, (stretches) over a number of the early years of life." He notes, too, that in studies of adults in mourning, these same expressions of hostility, ambivalence, and despair are found.

In commenting on Bowlby's paper, Spitz (1960) reports that no hostility is observed in children under one year of age following the loss of love object, so that this ambivalence may be partly a function of age. He also reports that it takes three to five months of separation to produce serious or irreversible consequences.

It is thus evident that although much is known about the descriptive aspects of grief and deprivation, much remains to be learned concerning their developmental aspects and their modification by experience. This represents an important area for future research.

The Dimension of Acceptance

One of the basic prototypic patterns of behavior found at all evolutionary levels is the ingestion or incorporation of food. Despite its universality and evident importance, comparatively little theoretical attention has been paid to it as a process having psychological significance. Studies using hunger as a motivator are, from the present point of view, more concerned with deprivation than they are with incorporation.

Proverbs, though, have not neglected it: for example, "A man is what he eats"; "I eat, therefore, I am"; "The greatest eaters are the best fighters"; "A good eater must be a good man"; "As a man eats so he works"; "I could eat him (or her) up."

Interestingly enough, this last expression is used in two contexts: in the first, to express hate toward someone, and in the second, to express love. In the first it would represent destruction through incorporation, while in the second case it implies acceptance or taking-in of a pleasure-producing object. Both imply extremely primitive prototypic types of reactions.

Psychoanalytic literature has actually recognized the importance of oral incorporation as a prototypic pattern. Schur (1960) points out that Freud used the model of a hungry infant as one of the prototypes of a traumatic situation and that Rapaport described this situation as "the conceptual model of psychoanalysis." Spitz (1957) examined this pattern in some detail. He reported the existence, in newborn infants, of a "rooting" pattern which he describes as a rotation of the infant's head from right to left and back again in rapid sweeps until the mouth touches the nipples of the breast and the lips close around it and sucking begins. The stimulus to rooting (which is a form of scanning behavior) is the touching of the face with the breast. One of the reasons for its significance is its reappearance in infants suffering loss of the mother as the "negative cephalogyric motion."

The rooting pattern is observable in infants immediately after birth and is reported to be demonstrable in three-month-old fetuses. It is a form of approach behavior which has survival value for the newborn infant. In psychoanalytic terms, it means *I want to take this into me,* and Spitz calls it a "behavior of affirmation." As the infant develops, the tactile (proximity) searching is abandoned and is replaced by visual (distance) searching which presumably, according to Spitz, becomes the prototype of mental activity. In general, in both man and animals, feeding represents a basis for socialization of the individual.

It thus seems evident that incorporative behavior is of psychological significance and that it has not been sufficiently studied. It should also be recognized that this prototypic pattern of acceptance has its opposite as do fear, anger, and joy, the opposite in this case being rejection, elimination, or spitting out behavior.

The Dimension of Disgust

The pattern of rejection or disgust is basically a form of riddance reaction by which the organism tries to eliminate a substance or object which has been incorporated. As the individual gains experience with objects, this pattern of behavior may occur in abbreviated form to the sight or smell of the object as a conditioned reaction. Although this is a basic protective mechanism and has considerable survival value for the individual, it has not been systematically studied.

One of the earliest descriptions was given by Darwin:

> The term "disgust" in its simplest sense, means something offensive to the taste. But as disgust also causes annoyance, it is generally accompanied by a frown, and often by gestures as if to push away or to guard oneself against the offensive object. . . . Extreme disgust is expressed by movements round the mouth identical with those preparatory to the act of vomiting. The mouth is opened widely, with the upper lip strongly retracted. . . . The partial closure of the eyelids or the turning away of the eyes or of the whole body, are likewise highly expressive of disdain. These actions seem to declare that the despised person is not worth looking at, or is disagreeable to behold. . . . Spitting seems an almost universal sign of contempt or disgust; and spitting obviously represents the rejection of anything offensive from the mouth.

Some years later, William James described disgust as an "incipient regurgitation or retching, limiting its expression often to the grimace of the lips and nose; satisfaction goes with a sucking smile, or tasting motion of the lips." James also drew attention to the fact that various taste sensations are often used to represent feelings or personality traits; for example, such terms as sweet, bitter, harsh, and so on.

This emotion seemed so important to the earlier commentators that McDougall assumed an instinct of repulsion and a corresponding emotion of disgust. He stated that disgust is produced by incorporating noxious stimuli of taste or smell and also by contact with slimy substances.

Thus we have such expressions of disgust in our language as *He is slimy* or *He gives me the creeps*, or *He makes me sick*, etc. Synonyms for disgust are dislike and distaste.

Reich (1949) described vomiting as a biologic expressive movement which acts convulsively to expel body contents. It is based on a peristaltic movement of the stomach and esophagus in the direction opposite to its normal function. In infants, vomiting is sometimes accompanied by diarrhea, another form of ejection.

In the studies of hypnotically induced emotion reported by Bull (1951), disgust produced two major reactions, one mainly visceral and the other mainly skeletal. These were 1) nausea, or near nausea, as if in preparation for vomiting, and 2) a turning away or averting reaction, as if to escape. The averting pattern was sometimes expressed by a drawing or pushing back or by a drawing up with the eyes looking down. It appeared that both disgust and fear included an averting reaction pattern.

Psychoanalytic writing has generally described this emotion in the context of fecal elimination and the anal stage of psychosexual development. Most psychoanalysts emphasize that certain personality traits such as compulsiveness, orderliness, and miserliness are connected with fixations at this stage of development. However, according to Suttie (1952), they do not give sufficient importance to the whole process of cleanliness training. Suttie believes that cleanliness training is more important in the development of social attitudes than even feeding for the following reasons:

(1) Evacuation is critical, orgastic in fact, whereas feeding brings a gradual detention of hunger.
(2) Evacuation is followed by the interesting and sensual experience of handling, washing, attention, and to begin with, by approval. Feeding, by contrast, is not accompanied by attention to the outside world (which indeed is all but invisible during feeding) and further it leads quietly and insensibly to sleep and not to the vivid waking experience of washing.

(3) As a rule, until weaning, the breast is always given willingly, whereas in our culture the maternal attitude to excreta is more equivocal, and the baby must feel her original appreciation change into intolerance—which must be anxiety-provoking in the highest degree.

(4) In the matter of suckling, the baby has little power to choose; hunger drives effectively, or death eliminates the recalcitrant. The experience of maternal pleasure-displeasure however can teach it sphincter control quite early, and this control affords the *very first experience of social power*. With this (limited, and to begin with, uncertain) power of affecting other people's *favor* expressions, there must go a sense of responsibility. Love is no longer unconditional, but it is "up to" the baby itself to "earn" it. Food . . . is never conditional in this sense until the period of sweet-giving or withholding. . . . This (view) does shift the main emphasis from its organic and sensual meaning to its social significance.

Whether Suttie's view of the social significance of the elimination function is correct in detail or not, it is evident that research should be directed at this problem. This represents a gap that needs to be filled by both clinical and experimental studies.

The Dimension of Surprise

All organisms are confronted at various times during their existence by novel stimuli. The pattern of reaction upon contact with such stimuli may be called orientation, startle, or surprise and is associated only with situations in which the stimuli are unevaluated, ambiguous, uncertain, excessively intense, or sudden.

Surprise or startle (at higher intensity) may be thought of as a biologically useful preparation for further activity, during which bodily arousal increases and all movements are held in check until the situation is in some way evalu-

ated. When the stimulus has been evaluated, the surprise
may quickly change to any other emotion, fear for example, if danger is evident, or joy if the stimulus is a source
of pleasure. Since novel stimuli in most natural environ-
ments are more likely to be associated with danger and
possible destruction, surprise is more likely to be associated
with fear than with other emotions. This connection has
been noted many times. For example, Darwin wrote,
"Fear is often preceded by astonishment, and is so far
akin to it, that both lead to the sense of sight and hearing
being instantly aroused. In both cases the eyes and mouth
are widely opened, and the eyebrows raised. . . ." Darwin also wrote that "attention . . . graduates into surprise; and this into astonishment; and this into stupefied
amazement. The latter frame of mind is closely akin to
terror." Nina Bull (1951) cites several other observers who
noted this same connection, although she also points out
that most situations are partly known and partly unknown,
so that surprise is frequently mixed both with fear and
with other emotions. The conclusion at which Bull arrives
is that "every sudden arrest of the attention is to be regarded as a general preparation for activity and involves a
posture which is maintained pending an investigation of
the startling stimulus."

This notion implies something which has also been
noted by other writers, that surprise associated with
a novel stimulus is quite often followed by an investigation of that stimulus and the more or less rapid development of expectations concerning it. Berlyne (1960), in his
analysis of the problems of conflict and curiosity, says
that "surprisingness . . . implies the existence of an expectation with which the (novel) stimulus disagrees." One
of his experiments showed that "surprising" figures (in a
series) elicited more investigatory reactions from human
adults than more familiar figures.

Dykman et al. (1959), in a study of reactions to novel
stimuli, report that although the orienting response and
the startle reflex are different at their extremes, they gradually merge into one another. "In a normal subject, whether

animal or human, a weak stimulus produces an orienting response and a strong stimulus a startle reflex."

Both these reactions are expressed through gross body patterns involving motor, autonomic, and subjective components. These include a very transient, postural, flexion reaction and a tightening of all musculature, which is completed within half a second; a postural reorientation which moves the receptors of the organism into a position which makes stimulus reception more favorable; an increase in autonomic arousal including cardiovascular and EEG changes, and breathing changes. Several studies reviewed by Dykman report a fairly rapid adaptation to the novel stimuli, often within 5 to 10 exposures.

The specific pattern in startle is presumably affected by a number of variables which have not been adequately studied, such factors, for example, as intensity of stimulus, degree of novelty of the stimulus, level of arousal of the organism, and, in humans, type of person. It was shown in two studies (Loomis, 1931, and Anna Freud and Burlingham, 1944) that the frequency and type of physical contact of children greatly affect their emotional behavior. Although the total number of physical contacts in children increased with age, there were wide individual differences, and early and extensive contact with other children was reported to increase aggressive responses. The startle reflex also has a developmental history, reportedly beginning at around the fourth month of life in humans.

Very little has been written either about the developmental aspects of surprise or startle or about its mixture with other emotions. One exception is a paper by Greenacre (1956) which discusses the emotion of awe, defined as a "complex state of dread mingled with veneration, usually associated with a feeling of strangeness or unfamiliarity." Greenacre reports that patients in analysis describe experiences of awe at the ages of 4 to 5, again at 6 to 7, and then later at adolescence. She also indicates that urinary problems of one sort or another are usually found in male patients who have strong feelings of phallic awe. This study suggests that surprise (like other primary emotions) may be combined with other body patterns and be reflected in certain persistent emotional attitudes. Darwin also commented on a mixed emotion related to surprise. He suggested that admiration consists of "surprise associated with some pleasure and a sense of approval." The emotion of surprise requires considerably more research before reliable generalizations can be made.

The Dimension of Expectation

The constant activity which apparently acts to keep the individual in contact with and informed about the environment is a basic prototypic pattern of behavior. This is "exploratory" behavior, and though it is seen universally in some form in all animals, it has not been systematically studied. "Exploratory behavior may also be thought of as reflecting a primary tendency of all tissues, including the sense organs and their central nervous connections towards functional expression. . . . Locomotor and manipulative exploration, being extensions of perception, would then be counted among the primary drives" (Nissen, 1951).

Earlier writers considered exploration a basic drive or instinct. For example, Tolman in 1923 wrote that "Manipulation or curiosity, assuming that there is such an innate propensity, would seem to be another original 'to get more of tendency. . . . (but) whereas love is a 'to get more of' by encouraging or enticing, curiosity is a 'to get more of' by examining, or exercising one's sense organs upon." Five years later in the Wittenberg Symposium, McDougall wrote, "The emotion-quality wonder accompanies always, in some degree, the impulse or desire to explore and to become better acquainted with some object . . . The process of exploration leads to the better comprehension of the nature of the object."

Somewhat earlier, Pavlov had already written about the investigatory or *what is it?* reflex observable in his experimental animals, which acts to orient receptor organs toward stimulus changes in the environment. He suggested that inquisitiveness in man might be an elaboration of this reaction (Dykman et al., 1959).

More recently Spitz (1957) suggested that rooting behavior in the newborn child is a form of exploratory behavior in that it samples the environment until need gratification is achieved. According to the psychoanalytic view, both perception and thought represent scanning and sampling processes requiring proportionately less muscular energy.

However only in recent years has exploration as a process been studied under controlled conditions. Berlyne (1960) summarized most of these studies and described some of the variables which have been found to influence such behavior. These include the novelty of the stimulus, its changeableness, complexity, intensity and contrast, and its affective value. Both the previous environmental conditions and the heredity of the organism are also believed to affect exploratory behavior. An experiment by Anderson (1938) revealed that rats who were highly exploratory in one test situation were generally highly exploratory in others. Berlyne also noted that animals with more highly developed nervous systems tend to show more investigatory behavior generally and that "the tendency to approach novel stimulus objects is universal within and among species and is evident early in life." Many studies show that the opportunity for exploratory behavior is itself a reward.

All these observations are consistent with the notion of exploration as a basic prototypic pattern. But like all the other prototypes already discussed, it changes its form of expression somewhat in the course of phylogenesis and ontogenesis and is often described by other names. It is variously called curiosity, expectation and play.

For example, Berlyne (1960) writes, "Human investigatory behavior includes much of the creative activity on which science, art, and entertainment depend. . . . In human beings, ludic (play) behavior includes everything that is classified as recreation, entertainment, or 'idle curiosity' as well as art, philosophy, and pure (as distinct from applied) science." Nissen (1951), in his *Handbook* article, suggests that play behavior serves a purpose in that it helps to develop an individual's perceptual and motor patterns. In the Wittenberg Symposium, Krueger (1928) makes essentially the same point, and Suttie (1952) points out that "Necessity is not the mother of invention; play is." There is a proverb which makes a similar point: "An hour of play discovers more than a year of conversation." It may be noted parenthetically that the Chinese word for play, *wan,* has a variety of special meanings including to be busy, to enjoy something, to trifle, to jest, to mock, to finger, examine, sniff at, and to feel.

The most elaborate discussion of the role of play is found in *Homo Ludens* by the historian Huizinga (1950). Huizinga says that:

> Play is older than culture, for culture, however inadequately defined, always presupposes human society, and animals have not waited for man to teach them their playing. We can safely assert, even, that human civilization has added no essential feature to the general idea of play. Animals play just like men.
> . . . Play is more than a mere physiological phenomenon or a psychological reflex. . . . The *fun* of playing resists all analysis, all logical interpretation. As a concept it cannot be reduced to any other mental category. . . . Here we have to do with an absolutely primary category of life, familiar to everybody at a glance right down to the animal level. . . .
> In myth and ritual the great instinctive forces of civilized life have their origin: law and order, commerce and profit, craft and art, poetry, wisdom and science. All are rooted in the primaeval soil of play.

Considering the suggested importance of play in human life, it is surprising and regrettable that relatively little study has been devoted to this question. One exception is the study by Bott (1934) which deals with the development of play behavior in young children. At the age of two years, half of a child's time is spent in apparently aimless activity and about one tenth of his time in constructive activity. By the age of five years, the child spends one third of his time aimlessly and one third constructively. Over this same period of time the amount of manipulative activity decreases while the amount of group playing increases. It is very likely that these early experiences have subtle but long-lasting effects that need to be studied through longitudinal experiments.

It is important to note that the exploration of the environment leads to the development of expectations. In Tolman's words (1945), "Successive re-presentations of arrays of environmental stimuli arouse in an organism . . . expectancies." The definition of expectancies "does not involve the question as to whether or not they are conscious." The existence of expectations in man and lower animals may be inferred on the basis of preparatory or avoidance responses or on the basis of the readiness to recognize or mistake stimuli (Berlyne, 1960). The recent tendency in comparative psychology, according to Nissen (1951), is "to ascribe some degree or kind of purpose, at least to the higher animals, as indicated by the use of such terms as anticipation, expectancy, and goal orientation."

It is of considerable importance to note that these expectancies are very closely related to the idea of learning and conditioning. Many investigators have pointed out the anticipatory nature of the classical conditioned reflex. This includes Pavlov, who described "signalizing" reflexes as anticipatory or preparatory motor attitudes (Bull, 1951).

Liddell (1950) suggested that the energy for the anticipatory reactions in conditioning does not come from the unconditioned reaction but rather from the general state of arousal, which he calls "vigilance." From his point of view, the reinforcement "validates the animal's expectation but does not supply the power for the expectant behavior." Regardless of the adequacy of this particular interpretation, it seems evident that conditioning may be thought of as a process of developing expectations, and that this process depends, at least in part, upon initial exploratory behavior, orienting reactions, play, or operant activity.

Expectancies are opposite in nature to surprises. That which is surprising cannot have been expected. An organism cannot be both surprised and expectant about the same thing at the same time. This notion of the opposite nature of surprise and expectancy is consistent with the several other opposites already described, that is, anger and fear, acceptance and rejection, joy and sadness.

In this and the preceding chapter, an attempt has been made to describe briefly the evolution of eight prototypic patterns of behavior which represent emotion dimensions applicable to all organisms. It is evident that the observations are scattered and, in some cases, tentative or cursory. But as Nissen (1951) points out, "The literature contains an amazingly small number of studies in comparative psychology—investigations in which two or more species have been compared directly." This implies that an extensive program of research should be developed to close the gaps in our knowledge concerning the characteristics of these eight primaries. Such a program of research should be concerned with the following kinds of problems:

1. How are the eight primary dimensions expressed at each phylogenetic level? How does the increasing differentiation of parts and specialization of function during evolution change the pattern of expression of destruction, protection, incorporation, exploration, etc?

2. How are the eight prototypic patterns expressed in newborn members of each species, and how do the patterns change during the course of individual development?

3. What is the influence of particular types of conditions or experiences, such as isolation, sensory deprivation, sensory loss, reinforcement, and punishment on the pattern of expression of the eight primaries?

4. What relation exists between particular neural structures and the forms of expression of the eight primary patterns?

5. How do the eight primary patterns interact, fuse, and mix?

These questions suggest a general orientation for subsequent research. Although there are many scattered observations concerning these questions, systematic research has hardly begun.

8

A Structural Model of the Emotions

Nowadays we do not ask whether a given theory or concept is true or false. We ask: Is it convenient or inconvenient; is it useful or not?
—NICOLAS RASHEVSKY

The preceding chapters have attempted to clarify and justify the concept of eight primary emotion dimensions which are prototypic patterns of behavior involved in biological adaptation at all evolutionary levels. These were designated as the dimensions of destruction, protection, incorporation, rejection, reproduction, deprivation, orientation, and exploration. These dimensions seem to represent bipolar factors or axes with destruction versus protection, incorporation versus rejection, reproduction versus deprivation, and orientation versus exploration. This becomes even clearer if we think of the names used to describe these primary emotions when expressed in humans. We think of joy as opposed to sadness, acceptance to disgust, anger to fear, and surprise to expectation. These designations are obviously tentative because of one very important fact, that is, the dependence on intensity of the names given to emotions. Thus the dimension of rejection would include such intensity levels as boredom, dislike, antipathy, disgust, repulsion, and loathing; the deprivation dimension, pensiveness, melancholy, sadness, and grief.

These two observations, that is, the bipolar nature of the primary emotions, and the implicit intensity dimension, suggest the need for some kind of structural model or analogue to represent the organization and properties of the emotions.

Such an analogue may be found in the theory of color mixture. McDougall (1921) noted this parallel many years ago:

> The color-sensations present, like the emotions, an indefinitely great variety of qualities shading into one another by imperceptible gradations; but this fact does not prevent us regarding all these many delicate varieties as reducible by analysis to a few simple primary qualities from which they are formed by fusion, or blending, in all proportions. Rather it is the indefinitely great variety of color qualities, their subtle gradations, and the peculiar affinities between them, that justify us in seeking to exhibit them as fusions in many different proportions of a few primary qualities. And the same is true of the emotions.

In order to develop this analogy, it is necessary to conceive of the primary emotions as hues which may vary in degree of intermixture (saturation) as well as intensity, and as arrangeable around an emotion-circle similar to a color-wheel. Primary emotions which are opposite each other on such an emotion-circle should be thought of as complementary in the sense that their mixture produces the psychic or biological equivalent of gray (which is obtainable by mixing complementary colors). There should be some kind of gradation of emotions around the circle, so that adjacent emotions are more similar than emotions which are more removed, just as adjacent colors are more similar than opposite ones. The analogy also implies that mixtures or combinations of these primary emotions in various proportions will produce all of the emotions which are known and described in life. Such a model, as suggested in Chapter 1, should provide us with answers to the many questions that may be posed about emotions and at the same time should act as an integrator of facts already known, a predictor of new relationships, a stimulator of research, and an incorporator, that is, it should show relationships between apparently diverse areas.

In the process of developing the most effective model of the emotions there are likely to be many trials and errors. Such a model can be established only by a series of successive approximations.

The Structural Model

A first approximation to a structural model of the emotions is presented in Figure 1. It shows the eight prototypic dimensions arranged somewhat like the sections of half an orange, with the emotion terms which designate each emotion at maximum intensity at the top. The vertical dimension represents intensity, or level of arousal, and ranges from a maximum state of excitement to a state of deep sleep at the bottom. The shape of the model implies that the emotions become less distinguishable at lower intensities. If we imagine taking successive cross-sections, we keep duplicating the emotion-circle with progressively milder versions of each of the primaries.

The arrangement of emotions around this circle is designed to place similar emotions near each other, so far as is known. Chapters 6 and 7 noted that several authors have commented on the similarity between joy and anger. Both are expansive, both involve outwardly directed activity, both involve vocalizations, etc. Other emotions which clearly belong together are surprise and fear, or joy and acceptance, or the negative emotions of grief and disgust.

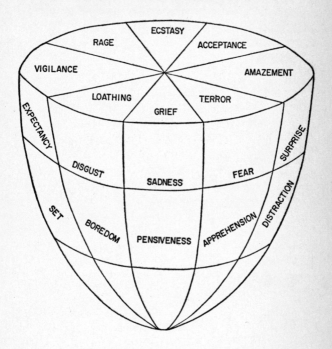

Fig. 1 A MULTI-DIMENSIONAL MODEL OF THE EMOTIONS

This arrangement around the emotion-circle is still tentative, depending for confirmation upon various kinds of studies of similarity of emotions. The problem may be studied from the point of view of facial expressions in emotion, linguistic similarity of connotations of emotion words, and physiological patterns of expression. Some data on the first two points have been collected and will be presented in the next chapter. The eventual decision on the arrangement will also depend upon the kind of internal consistency provided by one grouping rather than another.

The question of the exact form of the emotion-solid is an empirical problem which can be answered only by studies of level of arousal of the primary emotions. Since this is a subjective problem as well as a behavioral and physiological one, any one study of intensity of the primary emotions will provide only an approximation to the structure. With this limitation in mind, the following study of the judged intensity of emotion words was undertaken.

Experiment 1. The Judged Intensity of Emotion-Terms

A list of synonyms for each of the primary emotion dimensions was compiled, using as many as could be found in both the unabridged dictionary and *Roget's Thesaurus*. The number of synonyms found for each dimension varied. Three of the four emotions with the most synonyms are negative or unpleasant emotions, i.e., disgust, fear, and grief, thus suggesting that we are able to make finer discriminations with negative emotions than with positive ones.

These lists of synonyms were then presented to a group of thirty college students with the following instructions:

Here is a list of words describing emotions. Some of the words (such as surprise and startle) mean very much the same thing, but indicate a different level of intensity of the emotion. Please examine the entire list of emotions, and rate them in terms of the degree of intensity that they represent, using a scale of 1 to 11.
1 means a very, very *low* intensity of the emotion.
6 means a *moderate* level of intensity of the emotion.
11 means a very, very *high* level of intensity of the emotion. You may use any number from 1 to 11.

The mean judged intensity was then obtained for each of the terms. These data are summarized in Table 2, where, since some overlap is found, only words representing clear-cut differences are presented, ranging from highest to lowest.

Five of the emotions show maximum intensities in the range of 9 to 10, while the dimensions of *incorporation* and *exploration* are both relatively low on the intensity dimension. None of the minimum intensities are below a value of three, thus implying that no discriminations are made between emotions at very low intensity levels.

These intensity values might provide an approximate estimate of the shape of the emotion-solid. It is important to recognize that maximum intensity values vary for each of the primary dimensions and that we cannot match all emotions for intensity, since the maximum value for the incorporation dimension is only about 4. Similarly, the

Fig. 2 A CROSS-SECTION OF THE EMOTION-SOLID

TABLE 2

The mean judged intensity of synonyms for each of the eight primary emotion dimensions.

DIMENSIONS

DESTRUCTION	REPRODUCTION	INCORPORATION	ORIENTATION	PROTECTION	DEPRIVATION	REJECTION	EXPLORATION
Rage (9.90)	Ecstasy (10.00)	Admission (4.16)	Astonishment (9.30)	Terror (10.13)	Grief (8.83)	Loathing (9.10)	Anticipation (7.30)
Anger (8.40)	Joy (8.10)	Acceptance (4.00)	Amazement (8.30)	Panic (9.75)	Sorrow (7.53)	Disgust (7.60)	Expectancy (6.76)
Annoyance (5.00)	Happiness (7.10)	Incorporation (3.56)	Surprise (7.26)	Fear (7.96)	Dejection (6.26)	Dislike (5.50)	Attentiveness (5.86)
	Pleasure (5.70)			Apprehension (6.40)	Gloominess (5.50)	Boredom (4.70)	Set (3.56)
	Serenity (4.36)			Timidity (4.03)	Pensiveness (4.40)	Tiresomeness (4.50)	
	Calmness (3.30)						

orientation dimension has all of its emotion intensities ranging between 7 and 9; thus any of the forms of surprise occur at high intensity, if they occur at all. This is consistent with the various descriptions given in the previous chapter of surprise or startle as a sudden mobilization or orientation of the body in response to a novel stimulus.

Using these intensity judgments as a basis, it is possible to obtain groupings of emotion-terms representing the primary dimensions at nearly equal intensity levels. For example, rage, ecstasy, astonishment, panic, grief, and loathing all represent emotions judged to indicate intensity levels approximately between 9 and 10 on an 11-point scale. Anger, joy, surprise, fear, sorrow, disgust, and anticipation all represent medium levels of intensity somewhere between 7 and 8. The emotions of annoyance, pleasure, acceptance, timidity, pensiveness, boredom, and heedfulness represent low intensity levels of the primary dimensions, at about 4 to 5 on the 11-point scale. These groupings therefore represent approximate cross-sections of the emotion-solid and may be represented, as in Figure 2, for a medium intensity level.

The Mixing of Primary Emotions

With this model as the starting point, many interesting implications follow. We might begin by considering the various ways the primary emotions may be mixed in order to synthesize complex emotions. If we look at Figure 2, it is evident that any adjacent pair of primaries could be combined to form an intermediate mixed emotion, just as any two adjacent colors on the color-circle form an intermediate hue. A mixture of any two primaries may be called a dyad, of any three primaries, a triad. But these dyads and triads may be formed in different ways. If two adjacent primaries are mixed, the resulting combination may be called a primary dyad. Mixtures of two primary emotions which are once removed on the circle may be called secondary dyads, while mixtures of two primaries which are twice removed on the circle may be called tertiary dyads. The same general method of designation would apply to triads as well.

But how do we name the emotions which result from various mixtures? This problem is in a way similar to that faced by chemists at the beginning of the nineteenth century. Their task was to find ways of determining the elements present in any given compound. It took half a century of debate and experimentation before there was general agreement on the exact constituents of the simpler compounds. Even today, chemists do not know the exact formulas for all complex organic substances. Psychologists might well recognize the history of chemistry as a guide to what might be expected in their field.

That it is not always easy to name all of the combinations of emotions may be due to one or more reasons: perhaps our language does not contain emotion words for certain combinations, although other languages might; or perhaps certain combinations do not occur at all in human experience, just as chemical compounds can be formed only in certain limited ways; or perhaps the intensity differences involved in the combinations mislead us in trying to decide on a suitable name; or perhaps we have to make up our own names to describe certain compounds; perhaps we have not yet discovered all the emotional combinations of which man is capable. In chemistry, when a gap was discovered in the periodic table, it was still possible to discuss the properties of this hypothetical substance, to name it, and eventually to discover it.

One other important point might be made about the problem of naming emotion-compounds. This is a problem almost identical with that faced by the international conference which set out in 1931 to develop a system for the numerical specification of what a color looks like to the ordinary man or woman under a given set of conditions. Since there are certain differences in the reaction of individual observers, even after people with abnormal color vision have been eliminated, it was necessary to define a color match which would be acceptable to an average observer. This was done by defining how a "standard observer" sees any particular color. The average data from a small number of selected observers provided an imaginary standard observer and all results reported in the C.I.E. system are adjusted so as to satisfy the requirements of this standard observer. This is a system which has worked very well since 1931. Is it not possible to have the emotion-mixtures named by a group of specially selected standard observers?

Experiment 2. The Naming of Emotion-Mixtures

With the concept of standard observers as a basis, there are at least three possible approaches to the process of naming emotion mixtures.

1) Present a group of judges (standard observers) with all possible pairs of primary emotions and ask them to suggest an appropriate name for the resulting mixture.

2) Present a group of judges with a long list of emotion-names taken from our language and ask them to indicate which of the primaries are present.

3) Utilize the information from procedures 1) and 2) above and in addition consider the need for internal consistency, for example, that dyads which are opposite on the emotion circle should have opposing characteristics.

It was discovered that the first procedure listed above, that is, the introspective synthesis of primary emotions is a difficult task and one which produces more variability. Because of this, the major reliance has been placed on method 2. In this connection, a group of 34 judges were asked to examine a long list of emotion-terms in our language and to indicate which two or three of the primaries are components. In some cases, there was great consistency; in others, less. The following listing indicates those terms which appeared most frequently.

Primary Dyads
anger + joy = pride
joy + acceptance = love, friendliness

  acceptance + surprise = curiosity
  surprise + fear = alarm, awe
  fear + sorrow = despair, guilt
  sorrow + disgust = misery, remorse, forlornness
  disgust + expectancy = cynicism
  expectancy + anger = aggression, revenge, stubborn-
           ness

Secondary Dyads
  anger + acceptance = dominance (?)
  joy + surprise = delight
  acceptance + fear = submission, modesty
  surprise + sorrow = embarrassment, disappointment
  fear + disgust = shame, prudishness
  sorrow + expectancy = pessimism
  disgust + anger = scorn, loathing, indignation, con-
       tempt, hate, resentment, hostility
  expectancy + joy = optimism, courage, hopefulness,
       conceit

Tertiary Dyads
  anger + surprise = outrage, resentment, hate
  joy + fear = guilt
  acceptance + sorrow = resignation, sentimentality
  surprise + disgust = ?
  fear + expectancy = anxiety, caution, dread, coward-
       liness, distrust
  sorrow + anger = envy, sullenness
  disgust + joy = morbidness (?)
  expectancy + acceptance = fatalism

An examination of this list of tentative names for the
primary, secondary, and tertiary dyads reveals several
interesting things. First of all, it was possible to find
emotion-names for each of the mixtures of primary dyads,
but not for one pair of the secondary dyads and not for
two (at least) of the tertiary dyads. This suggests that
mixtures of emotions which are more widely separated on
the emotion-circle are harder to imagine or less likely to
be experienced than those which are closer. What name

shall be given to mixtures composed of surprise + disgust or even disgust + joy? These are certainly logical possibilities but they apparently occur rarely, if at all. If we think of this listing as being analogous to the periodic table in chemistry, we may consider these empty spaces as rare mixtures whose properties can still be estimated and which may yet be discovered or produced.

Just as opposite colors, when mixed in equal intensity, act to neutralize one another to produce gray, so too do opposite emotions, when occurring simultaneously in equal intensity, act to inhibit or neutralize each other. The result of a tendency to accept and, simultaneously, to reject leads to conflict and immobilization of action; similarly with the tendencies to approach or withdraw, destroy or protect, expand or contract. By the same reasoning, any combination of emotions which are nearly opposite leads to greater conflict and immobilization than combinations of adjacent emotions. This would imply that the tertiary dyads involve mixtures with more conflict than other types of dyads. This prediction is certainly borne out by the listing of dyads. Compare the tertiary dyads of resentment, hate, resignation, anxiety, distrust, envy, morbidness, and fatalism with the primary dyads of pride, love, curiosity, alarm, despair, misery, cynicism, and aggression. The latter listing refers to more-or-less normal emotions of everyday life, while the former listing refers to the clinical or pathological emotions. This is shown in Table 3.

Table 3 has been modified somewhat from the earlier listing of dyads to provide maximum internal consistency. It would be expected, for example, that a given emotion mixed with two opposites should produce mixtures which also tend to be opposite. Thus expectancy mixed with joy produces optimism, but when it is mixed with its opposite, sorrow, it produces pessimism. By the same reasoning, if acceptance + fear produces submission, then acceptance + anger should produce dominance. Surprise + joy produces delight and surprise + sorrow produces disappointment. The use of such reasoning in naming the emotion mixtures provides greater coherence in the model as a

TABLE 3

Primary, secondary, and tertiary dyads.

PRIMARY DYADS	SECONDARY DYADS	TERTIARY DYADS
pride	———*	resentment (outrage)*
love	delight	guilt
curiosity	submission	resignation
alarm	disappointment	———
despair	shame	anxiety (dread)
misery	scorn (contempt)	sullenness (envy)
cynicism	optimism	———
aggression	pessimism	fatalism

* The terms in parentheses are alternative designations of the emotion mixture. The dash indicates that no suitable name has been found.

whole. It may be noted, parenthetically, that some of the variation in names for particular mixtures probably relates to the differing interpretations of intensity levels, as well as differences in the personal experiences of the judges.

Emotion Mixtures as Personality Traits

An examination of the listing of dyads shows that many of them represent feeling states which would seem to be relatively persistent. Emotions like pride, aggression, submission, and optimism are usually long-lasting, and in fact are often called personality traits. We talk of proud, aggressive, submissive, and optimistic people. This suggests that the formation of personality traits is related to the development of mixed emotions, and since some degree of conflict is connected with the mixing of emotions, all personality traits imply components in greater or lesser conflict. Since emotions are reactions to specific kinds of situations which call out the response of destruction, protection, rejection, etc., it may be concluded that *persisting situations which produce mixed emotions produce personality traits.*

This is an important implication of the theory and is completely consistent with some central psychoanalytic concepts. Fenichel (1946) has expressed this in the following ways:

> Character traits are the precipitates of instinctual conflicts. . . . In character attitudes, conflicts between impulses and fears may be relatively frozen. . . . This then is the situation. Once there was a conflict. The individual withdrew from this struggle by means of a permanent ego alteration. The forces that at one time opposed each other are now wasted in the useless and rigid defensive attitudes of the ego; the conflict has become latent.

In other words, a conflict between two or more emotions produces a new unique personality trait or character attitude which persists in time. This clarifies an issue raised by Rapaport (1950) in Landauer's (1938) terms: "Are the affects really reactions? In children we still see them as such. But in later life anxiety is apparently continuous in the anxious-minded, the pessimist is permanently melancholy and the cheerful man consistently buoyant. *How does an isolated reaction become a continuous state?*" (italics added). The answer proposed here is that persisting situations which produce conflicts of emotions produce personality traits.

This raises the very interesting research question of what specific conditions of life bring about the mixing of emotions and the development of personality traits. Here too the psychoanalytic literature has many suggestive observations. To cite just a few of Fenichel's, "Stubbornness is a passive type of aggressiveness, developed where activity is impossible. . . . Compulsion neurotics are frequently particularly polite, accommodating and considerate. These

are reaction formations that oppose aggressive tendencies.
. . . Exceptional oral deprivation determines a pessimistic
(depressive) or sadistic attitude." Fenichel suggests four
general factors which determine the fixation of character
attitudes: 1) the nature of the instinctual impulses that
have to be warded off; 2) the time when the decisive
conflict was experienced; 3) the content and intensity of
the frustrations and the nature of the frustrating factors;
and 4) whether substitute gratifications are available.
These concepts are closely related to some of those
presented in connection with the frustration-aggression
hypothesis (Berkowitz, 1958). It should also be possible
in time to incorporate many of the concepts concerning
conflict which have been developed through laboratory
studies of animals and humans.

There are many research possibilities open in the study
of emotion-mixing. One which concerns the analysis of
emotion-components in personality traits has been studied
in the following way.

Experiment 3. The Analysis of Personality Traits*

This study is an extension of Experiment 2. A much longer
list of trait names was used and a greater range of intensities for the emotion-components was included.

Starting with Allport's list of over 18,000 so-called trait
names, an extensive preliminary reduction took place on
the basis of a series of criteria. These were: 1) that the
trait should refer to a persistent rather than a transient
characteristic of the individual; 2) that it reflect how the
individual acts toward other people rather than how they
act toward him, and 3) that it not include physical
characteristics, moral attitudes, intellectual capacities or
aptitudes, or social status. The application of these criteria
reduced Allport's list to about 450 trait names. These
were then grouped by other judges into categories which
were similar, producing 202 groups. One word from
each of the 202 groups was then selected to represent the
group, thus leaving 120 words.

* This study was done with the assistance of Henry Bender.

Half of these trait names were then given to a group of college students and half to a group of public school teachers. The judges were asked to choose the emotion-components of each of the traits from a list of 8 groups of 2 or 3 words, each representing different intensity levels of the primary emotion dimensions. These eight groups were as follows:

1. pleasure, joy, ecstasy
2. acceptance, incorporation
3. surprise, astonishment
4. timidity, fear, panic
5. pensiveness, sorrow, grief
6. boredom, disgust, loathing
7. heedfulness, anticipation, expectation
8. annoyance, anger, rage.

It will be noted that, except for 2 and 3, each group represents low, medium, and high intensity emotion words as previously scaled in Experiment 1.

The results of this experiment provide us with a detailed quantitative statement of the intensity of each of the emotion-components in the selected personality traits. For example, Table 4 is a brief list of some of the personality traits with the two most consistently reported components. Notice that several personality traits may have the same two principal dimensions as components, but at different intensity levels. For example, the traits sarcastic, cruel, spiteful, vicious, and rebellious all have as two main components the dimensions of destruction and rejection. But sarcastic is judged as having a low intensity anger and a high intensity digust; cruel as having a high intensity anger and high intensity disgust; spiteful, a medium intensity disgust and a medium intensity anger, etc. This procedure thus provides a possible basis for making finer discriminations between personality traits, as well as increased insight into the component elements of human personality.

It should be evident that three emotions can be mixed, as well as two. The problem of naming them becomes pro-

TABLE 4

*The emotion-components in some
personality traits.*

TRAIT	EMOTION-COMPONENTS	
	First choice	*Second choice*
Sarcastic	Annoyance	Loathing
Cruel	Rage	Loathing
Spiteful	Disgust	Anger
Vicious	Rage	Loathing
Rebellious	Rage	Disgust
Anxious	Anticipation	Fear
Cautious	Timidity	Heedfulness
Servile	Fear	Acceptance
Obedient	Acceptance	Timidity
Docile	Timidity	Acceptance
Forlorn	Sorrow	Timidity
Shy	Timidity	Fear
Pessimistic	Sorrow	Fear
Hopeful	Anticipation	Pleasure
Sullen	Sorrow	Annoyance
Sentimental	Pensiveness	Pleasure

portionately greater and the ambiguities increase, a fact
consistent with our daily experience. If someone asks, *how
do you feel?*, it is relatively easy to describe a single
dominant feeling, more difficult if two emotions are
present, and harder still with three.

But it should be clear by now that the assumption of
the mixing of eight primaries will permit the synthesis of
the manifold emotions which our language describes.
Eight primaries lead to 24 dyads and 32 triads, a total of
56 different emotions at one intensity level. If we assume
even four discriminable levels of intensity, this would
produce over 224 combinations of emotions, and if we
assume further interactions between the intensity levels,
thousands of combinations are possible. Yet by analysis,

it is possible to reduce all these to combinations of only eight qualitatively different dimensions. With this theory, instead of asserting that many different kinds of anger or fear exist, corresponding to different situations or persons, such things as a "pale anger" or a "resentful depression" are conceived of as mixed emotions. Thus the many complex emotions of life may be simplified in terms of a theory having a few basic assumptions.

In the next chapter, several studies which have developed from the theory will be described. A concluding chapter presents some implications and speculations, as well as a series of tentative answers to the list of questions at the beginning of the book.

9

Some Experimental Studies Based on the Theory

Many of us are harassed by relentless and importunate cravings for scientific maturity, which incline us to leap over all the tedious stages of observation, description, and classification through which chemistry and all the biological and medical sciences have passed . . .

—HENRY A. MURRAY

In the preceding chapter, three studies were briefly described which were concerned with the scaling of emotion words for intensity, the naming of emotion mixtures, and the determination of emotion-components of personality traits. In this chapter a number of studies will be described which have been based upon the theory; they range from studies of facial expression, to children's perception of primary emotions, to the semantic differential analysis of emotion terms. The studies have been included in this chapter in order to illustrate the broad range of applicability of the theory, and its fruitfulness for stimulating specific research projects. This by no means covers the possible range of studies. Some of these have already been suggested in Chapter 7 and others will be suggested in the following chapter.

Experiment 4. The Analysis of Facial Expressions

This experiment was concerned basically with the communication of emotions by facial expressions (Hill, 1955). This problem has a long history which, unfortunately, is not marked by consistent reports for several reasons:

1. In studies which use posed facial expressions, there is serious question as to what a "correct" judgment is, since the actor doing the posing often uses somewhat meaningless phrases to describe these posed emotions, *e.g.*, breathless interest, religion, reverential, affable, justified anger, altruistic pride, or self-sufficiency.

2. Judges often report that more than one emotion is expressed by the face and that a single descriptive adjective is not adequate.

3. When judges are allowed to use any descriptive emotion term they wish, a bewildering array of expressions results which is difficult to classify.

4. When restricted categories of emotion names are used, there is usually no theoretical rationale for choosing one group of emotion names rather than another.

These same problems also apply when so-called natural or unposed expressions are used.

A reasonable attempt at solving these problems might be made by using photographs or drawings of parts of the face. Several studies of this sort have been made (Buzby, 1924, Frois-Wittman, 1930, Hanawalt, 1944) but the results are somewhat inconsistent on the question of the relative importance of different parts of the face for each emotion.

Method. The study reported here utilized posed facial expressions of parts of the face but attempted to avoid all four of the problems listed above. The basic procedure was to require two subjects, a man and a woman, to pose their faces into all of the logically possible partial expressions the face could assume, without any reference to emotions per se. For example, the forehead can assume three expressions: being raised, frowning, and frowning and being raised simultaneously. The eyes can assume expressions in which they are slightly, moderately, or widely open, and in which they are looking up, down, or to the side. The mouth may have various expressions relating to circular or elliptical shapes and to crescents and inverted crescents.

Color photographs were taken of all these expressions and the resulting slides prepared in such a way as to present only the desired part of the face. By this method, 26 partial facial expressions were obtained for each subject.

These slides were then shown to a group of 51 evening college students in a psychology class. The students were given a sheet with printed instructions and a list of the eight primary emotions of the theory at medium intensity levels, and were requested to judge each partial expression only in terms of this list of eight emotions. A first and second choice was requested.

Results. Using the most frequently given responses as a basis, a composite picture of the facial expressions for the eight primary emotions may be synthesized. The dominant features for each emotion as determined by very consistent responses are as follows: for acceptance, the mouth; for surprise, the eyes, mouth, and forehead; for fear, the eyes; for sadness, the eyes; for disgust, the mouth; for expectancy, the eyes and mouth; for anger, the mouth; and for joy, the mouth. In summary, the greatest consistency of judgments were for mouth expressions. Joy is characterized by an upturned crescent, disgust by an inverted crescent, and anger by an elliptically shaped mouth.

A further question concerns the degree of overlap between the different facial expressions. In other words, since the judges had a first and second choice, which pairs of emotions were most likely to be used together? The results indicate that surprise and fear, joy and acceptance, and anger and disgust are most often given together as first and second choices. The second choice for expectancy tends to be scattered among the various alternatives. In the cases where fear was found as the most frequent first choice, the second choices in order of frequency were anger and disgust. When sadness was found as the most frequent first choice, acceptance, disgust, and anger were given as most frequent second choices, in that order.

These results are largely consistent with the expectations based on the theory in terms of the ordering of primaries around the emotion-circle. Surprise is next to fear and joy is next to acceptance, as predicted. Sadness is next to disgust, as predicted, except for its confusion with acceptance. This may have been due to the judges' misinterpretation of the meaning of acceptance; they may have thought of it in the sense of resignation and hence sadness.

The major discrepancies between theory and data are the difficulty of relating expectancy to any consistent second choice and the tendency to confuse fear with both anger and disgust. This confusion did not occur with any appreciable frequency, however.

These results should be thought of primarily as having heuristic value in making the theory seem plausible, not as a method of proof. This is an important point because the assumed primaries are hypothetical constructs, states of the organism as a whole, and are therefore only partially reflected by differences of facial expression. There are undoubtedly many differences between the primaries besides facial expression, and thus there will be no simple one-to-one connection between facial expression alone and the sequence of ordering around the emotion-circle. Only by a series of successive approximations can we construct a composite picture of these primaries as a totality.

There is, in addition, another source of variation to help account for the results: *i.e.*, that the primaries can exist in different degrees or intensities. Some of the judges may have thought of anger as rage and some as irritation or annoyance and thus interpreted the pictures differently.

It might be noted, parenthetically, that the composite emotion expressions developed by this method are very similar to those of Thompson (1941), Hanawalt (1944), and Frois-Wittman (1930).

In conclusion, Hill's study (1955), which was designed to avoid several sources of error commonly found in studies of facial expression, provided results largely consistent with the theory.

Experiment 5. The Synthesis of Facial Expressions*

Method. This experiment was developed as a sequel to the previous one. All of the expressions used in the slides of the earlier study were made into 8 x 10 black and white glossy prints and mounted on cardboard. Each picture was then cut into three portions, a forehead, an eye, and a mouth portion, and those expressions then selected which had been used in the prior study. There were thus 28 partial facial expressions, 4 of the forehead, 10 of the eyes, and 14 of the mouth, each approximately 3 x 8 inches in size.

These pictures were then placed in rows on a table and shown to 28 adult judges, 14 males and 14 females, who were asked to regroup these pictures to form a whole face to represent certain emotions. The subjects were to pick one forehead expression, one eye expression, and one mouth expression and try to represent the stated emotion. The emotion names used represented the eight primary emotion dimensions of the theory at a moderate intensity level: anger, fear, joy, sadness, disgust, expectation, surprise, and acceptance. (A few additional terms were used as part of another problem.)

Results. In comparing the results of this study with that described previously, a fair amount of agreement ap-

* These data were collected and analyzed by Betty Montgomery, a graduate student at the University of Cincinnati.

peared. For example, an eye expression called surprise in the analysis study was used most frequently to construct surprise in the synthesis study. This kind of agreement occurred with certain forehead, eye, and mouth expressions and particularly with the emotions of surprise, disgust, and acceptance. Agreement on first, second, or third choices occurred on 23 out of 26 of the partial facial expressions used in both studies. (This agreement could have been even higher were it not for the fact that some additional emotion-names were used, such as mirth, determination, love, and so on, in order to test simultaneously some of Schlosberg's conceptions. This increased the spread of judgments over a larger number of verbal categories and may thereby have reduced reliability somewhat.)

If the data are examined from the point of view of overlap of judgments for different emotions, the following picture emerges.

1. The emotions of joy, acceptance, sadness and expectation are all most frequently constructed with a normal, i.e., uncreased forehead. Surprise, fear and disgust have raised foreheads, while anger is depicted frowning.

2. Since there are ten different eye expressions with an attendant increase in variability, it is more appropriate to use the two most frequently used expressions for evaluation than the one most frequently used. From this point of view, joy overlaps with acceptance, surprise with fear, disgust with anger, and expectation with anger.

3. The most divergent results appear in considering mouth expressions. The most frequent overlap is between sadness and anger. If the second most frequent choices are included, then surprise, fear, expectation, and anger all overlap. Again this result is probably related to the fact that there are 14 possible choices for mouth expressions, which tends to increase variability.

These findings, at least for forehead and eye expressions, are consistent with the expectations of the theory. Divergences from theory may be accounted for partly at least by the differing meanings of words like anger fear, acceptance, etc., to the different judges. It will be necessary in follow-up studies to anchor the meanings of these terms more precisely, as well as to specify and study facial expressions for different intensity levels of the primaries. These two studies taken jointly provide some insight into the facial patterns associated with the primary emotions in humans, and could, with suitable refinements, give valuable information about the similarity of primary emotions.

Experiment 6. Children's Perceptions of the Primary Emotions*

Another approach to determining the empirical properties of the primary emotions in humans is through the perceptions of children. The verbal description of emotional states must be learned through experience, and it is an interesting problem to determine the particular conditions under which a child learns appropriate uses of such terms as anger, disgust, and sadness.

Method. This experiment was carried out using a large number of public school children ranging in age from about 8 years to 11 years who were in the third to the fifth grades. There were 110 in the third grade, 88 in the fourth grade, and 60 in the fifth grade. In each grade, the number of boys was about equal to the number of girls.

The children were asked to write down how they feel when they are angry, frightened, sad, disgusted, or joyful. They were also asked to briefly indicate the cause of their feeling and what they usually do when they feel that way. Finally they were asked to draw pictures expressing each of these five emotions. A set of drawings from one of the children is shown in Figure 3.

Results. The results of this experiment should answer two questions: how do children describe these primary emo-

* These data were gathered with the assistance of Esther Rolnick, a graduate student at Yeshiva University.

tions in terms of cause, feeling state, and action and is there a change with age? The analysis will be mainly descriptive because of the variety of answers, and only the findings for the third and fifth grades will be summarized.

Joy   Anger

Fear   Disgust   Sadness

Fig. 3   A CHILD'S DRAWING OF FIVE PRIMARY EMOTIONS

THE EMOTION OF ANGER

The third grade. The children usually said they felt "mad" and wanted to fight. The most commonly described causes

were being hit or teased, being prevented from doing
something, losing something, or breaking a toy.

The fifth grade. The children said they felt mad, vicious,
very frustrated, hot in your throat. One said, "You feel
like you want to push the world out of your life," another
that he felt "dislike toward the person." Many indicated
a desire to hit or kill someone else. The sources of anger
were: being teased, yelled at, hit, in a fight, or "when
everything goes wrong," "when nobody agrees with you,"
"when someone takes something from you," or "when
somebody breaks something." One wrote: "I feel hot,
mean, and like tearing everything apart."

Conclusions: 1) The number of descriptive terms used to
indicate the state of anger seems to increase with age.
2) The intensity of the reaction appears to increase with
age and even includes the urge to kill. 3) The situations
producing anger all involve some frustration, although
the variety of frustrating situations increases with age.

THE EMOTION OF FEAR

The third grade. The children said that in fear they felt
like running away or like crying. One wrote, "I would
like to jump out of my skin." Another noted that his
"heart beats." The causes of fear are: being alone, being
in the dark, "scary" movies, lightning, and thunder.

The fifth grade. The children described their states as:
very shivery, scary and chilly, cold and nervous, afraid
something terrible will happen. One reported that he
starts perspiring. The causes are: darkness, animals, bad
dreams, "big kids," bad report cards, having a test in
school, and "when I do something wrong."

Conclusions: 1) The number of descriptive terms used to
indicate fear seems to increase with age, with more body
states being mentioned. There are feelings of retreat,
shakiness, chills, and stiffness. 2) The sources of fear remain the same except that the 10- to 11-year-olds add

some situations connected with school and other social situations.

THE EMOTION OF SADNESS

The third grade. The children usually said they felt "not happy" and wanted to cry, or that they felt lonely. Sadness is produced "when someone dies," "when someone leaves you or moves," "when people do not like me," or "when there is no one to talk to." One wrote: "I feel lost, a nothingness."

The fifth grade. The children report feeling unhappy, sorry, lonely, disappointed, bad, low down and miserable, a desire to cry, "like you can't do anything," that "there is nothing to do," or that everything is going wrong. The causes again are: when someone (usually a friend or relative) dies, moves away, or gets hurt, "when nobody likes you," "when you want something special and you didn't get it," or "when something can't happen."

Conclusions: 1) Sadness seems to be associated with experiences of loss or loneliness at all ages. 2) The range of descriptive terms increases with age.

THE EMOTION OF DISGUST

The third grade. The terms sick, horrible, and "I have to throw up" were used to describe this state. It was produced by seeing someone else throwing up, or by "ugly things," "crushed things," or "bad looking things." Some said it occurred "when I get food I don't like" or "when I can't stand something." (A number of children did not answer this question.)

The fifth grade. The children described their feelings with such terms as: fed-up, angry, disappointed, mad, hateful, nauseous, sore, sick and tired, annoyed, squirmy, disgraced. The expressions used to describe causes of disgust were quite varied at this age and the more common ones are cited in full: "when you hate something, you can't stand it," "when you try to help someone who doesn't want help," "when I have a fight with someone," "when someone doesn't let you play," "when you feel that nobody likes you," "when I can't do something I want to do." There were only a few references to food or vomiting as causes of disgust as compared to the third grade. For the first time, several children wrote that it would be caused by the bad smell of something.

Conclusions: 1) Disgust is clearly associated with an urge to vomit at younger ages but with strong feelings of anger for older children. Perhaps this is an illustration of children reacting to one emotional state with another, causing a mixture or fusion of the two. 2) In younger children, particular foods or food habits were major sources of disgust, while for older children, food plays a relatively small role and social situations of various kinds became important causes. Bad odors are mentioned for the first time as causes at older ages.

THE EMOTION OF JOY OR PLEASURE

The third grade. The children reported feeling happy or good and that this occurs when they get a toy or something good, or "when I go on a trip."

The fifth grade. The children described feeling happy, full of fun, good, merry and jolly, fine, relaxed, some felt like laughing and some said they liked everybody. These feelings are produced by gifts, birthdays, when something good happens, "when someone shows me they like me," "when everything goes right," and by good marks in school.

Conclusions: 1) The number of terms descriptive of joy increases with age. 2) So, too, do the reports of overt manifestations of the feeling. 3) Getting something desired seems to be the major source of pleasure at all ages.

SUMMARY

This study provides important information on the perceived feelings and causes of five of the primary emotions in children and shows certain interesting trends with age.

This kind of information, when expanded over wider age ranges and additional emotions, should increase the adequacy of our approximation to the properties of the eight primary emotion dimensions.

Experiment 7. The Analysis of Emotions by the Use of the Semantic Differential*

Since emotions are described by words which have a semantic history and connectedness of their own, it should be possible to apply some of the techniques developed for the study of language meanings to the analysis of emotion words. One such technique developed in recent years, particularly by Osgood, Suci, and Tannenbaum (1957), is the "semantic differential," which approaches the meanings of words psychologically instead of grammatically.

This approach finds that it is possible to determine the connotative meanings of words by having judges check which of a standard series of bipolar adjectives apply to the words in question. The bipolar terms are usually separated by a seven-point scale so that an intensity as well as a direction estimate may be determined.

The adjective scales used by Osgood were obtained through a series of factor-analytic studies which isolated three major factors: an evaluation factor (illustrated by such adjective pairs as good-bad, pleasant-unpleasant, and clean-dirty); a potency factor (illustrated by strong-weak, large-small, and heavy-light), and an activity factor (illustrated by fast-slow, active-passive, and sharp-dull).

Many studies have used this procedure to determine word meanings but one of particular relevance here was reported by Block (1957). A group of male and a group of female college students were asked to rate fifteen emotions, selected a priori, on twenty of Osgood's adjective scales. The results for each emotion were put in rank-order and a factor analysis performed to determine the inter-

* These data were gathered and analyzed with the assistance of Henry Bender, a graduate student at Hofstra College.

correlations between the emotions. This was done separately for men and women.

The analysis revealed three major factors: a pleasantness-unpleasantness dimension (love vs. grief, anticipation vs. guilt, contentment vs. worry, etc.); a level of activation dimension (anger, pride and elation vs. nostalgia and boredom), and a factor called interpersonal relatedness illustrated by such emotions as sympathy, nostalgia, and grief. No differences were found between men and women in their judgments.

The first two factors are clearly identical with Osgood's evaluation and activity dimensions; the third one seems to be unique to these particular data. Unfortunately no attempt was made by Block to assess the degree of similarity of the different emotions, nor does he provide any rationale for the particular choice of emotion words used.

Method. Twenty emotion words were chosen to represent the eight primary dimensions at several different intensity levels. The emotion names chosen were: apprehension, fear, terror; surprise, astonishment; acceptance, receptivity; joy, ecstasy; annoyance, anger, rage; hopefulness, expectancy, vigilance; disgust, loathing; pensiveness, sadness, grief. From Osgood's list of adjective-pairs, 34, representing each of the three factor dimensions, were selected and presented to sixteen judges, all graduate psychology students. They were asked to judge the applicability of the 34 dimensions to the emotion words, using a seven-point scale. The adjective-pairs used are presented in Table 5.

Results. One point which should be clarified before proceeding concerns the significance of a neutral judgment on any scale. In the standard instructions to the judges, they are told, "If you consider the concept to be *neutral* on the scale, both sides of the scale *equally associated* with the concept, or if the scale is completely irrelevant, unrelated to the concept, then you should place your check-mark in the middle space." What this means is that a judgment at or near the center of the seven-point scale is essentially *indeterminate* in meaning because it may imply either that

TABLE 5

The adjective-pairs used in the semantic differential study of emotion words.

good .... bad		graceful ..... awkward	
harmonious . dissonant		sociable ..... unsociable	
high .... low		pleasurable .. painful	
strong ...... weak		hard .... soft	
masculine ... feminine		constrained .. free	
stable ...... changeable		hot .... cold	
sharp ...... blunt		angular ..... rounded	
pungent .... bland		youthful .... mature	
symmetrical . asymmetrical		formed ..... formless	
public ...... private		unusual ..... usual	
periodic .... erratic		complete .... incomplete	
wet .... dry		heavy ...... light	
interesting .. boring		excitable .... calm	
straight ..... curved		constricted .. spacious	
complex .... simple		active ...... passive	
large .... small		excited ..... depressed	
healthy ..... sick		fast .... slow	

the word is equally associated with both ends of the scale, or that the scale is completely irrelevant. Because of this, it seemed desirable and necessary to use judgments which clearly indicated that one end of the scale or the other was relevant. It was therefore decided to use in the analysis only those mean judgments which were 3.0 or less or 5.0 or more on the seven-point scale, thus omitting from consideration the middle or ambiguous portion of the scale.

On this basis, an immediate finding was that some of the scales seemed irrelevant to any of the emotions. For example, the scales wet-dry, straight-curved, complex-simple, youthful-mature, and formed-formless, were always judged in the middle (3.0-5.0) portion of the scale. Some of the other scales, such as symmetrical-asymmetrical and periodic-erratic, were rarely used outside of the middle range. Thus it is obvious that certain of the semantic differential scales are more relevant to the description of emotions than others.

Consistent with this observation was the fact that certain descriptive adjectives were frequently judged at the extremes for many different emotions. These pairs included the following: good-bad, pleasure-pain, excited-depressed, and active-passive.

It is of even greater interest that an increase in the intensity of emotion within any dimension produces a systematic change in the ratings applied to the adjective-pairs. This is illustrated by the ratings for the different emotions.

The mean judgments for the protection or "fear" dimension are as follows:

Apprehension	*Fear*	*Terror*
Bad (2.9)	Bad (2.6)	Bad (1.9)
Dissonant (3.0)	Dissonant (2.4)	Dissonant (2.2)
Painful (2.7)	Painful (1.8)	Painful (1.4)
Excitable (5.1)	Excitable (5.8)	Excitable (6.4)
	Constricted (3.0)	Constricted (1.8)
	Awkward (2.8)	Awkward (2.5)
	Constrained (5.1)	Constrained (5.0)
	Heavy (5.1)	Heavy (5.4)
		High (5.4)
		Strong (5.2)
		Changeable (2.7)
		Sharp (5.5)
		Pungent (5.6)
		Asymmetrical (2.9)
		Erratic (2.9)
		Large (5.2)
		Sick (2.9)
		Unsociable (2.7)
		Hard (5.4)
		Angular (5.1)
		Unusual (5.3)
		Active (5.2)
		Excited (5.9)
		Fast (5.3)

This compilation shows very clearly that as the intensity of the emotion increases two things happen: first, there is an increase in the extremism of judgments, and second, there is an increase in the number of adjective-pairs to which extreme judgments are made. Thus there are four adjective-pairs for which extreme judgments are made for apprehension, eight for fear, and twenty-four for terror. At the same time, the range of mean judgments is 2.7-5.1 for the low intensity emotion, 1.8-5.8 for the medium intensity emotion, and 1.4-6.4 for the high intensity emotion.

These general trends, so clearly shown for the protection dimension, are also found more-or-less clearly for the other dimensions.

ORIENTATION DIMENSION

Surprise	*Astonishment*
High (6.6)	————
Changeable (2.8)	Changeable (2.9)
Pleasurable (5.3)	————
Excitable (5.7)	Excitable (5.7)
Active (5.1)	Active (5.4)
Excited (5.7)	Excited (5.7)
Fast (5.1)	Fast (5.1)
	Interesting (5.3)
	Sharp (5.1)
	Unusual (2.7)

INCORPORATION DIMENSION

Receptivity	*Acceptance*
Good (5.4)	Good (5.4)
Harmonious (5.6)	Harmonious (5.5)
Sociable (5.4)	Sociable (5.6)
Pleasurable (5.3)	Pleasurable (5.1)
	Complete (5.1)
	Healthy (5.3)
	Calm (2.9)

REPRODUCTION DIMENSION

Joy	*Ecstasy*
Good (6.4)	Good (5.9)
Harmonious (6.2)	Harmonious (5.3)

REPRODUCTION DIMENSION

Joy	*Ecstasy*
High (6.2)	High (5.7)
Strong (5.7)	Strong (5.5)
Sharp (5.0)	Sharp (5.5)
Interesting (5.1)	Interesting (5.9)
Healthy (5.4)	Healthy (5.1)
Sociable (5.5)	Sociable (5.0)
Pleasurable (6.5)	Pleasurable (6.3)
Complete (5.3)	Complete (5.2)
Excitable (5.2)	Excitable (6.3)
Spacious (5.6)	Spacious (5.6)
Active (5.6)	Active (5.6)
Excited (6.1)	Excited (7.0)
	Fast (5.0)
	Unusual (2.7)
	Hot (5.1)
	Free (2.2)
	Large (5.4)
	Private (2.9)
	Pungent (5.3)

DESTRUCTION DIMENSION

Annoyance	*Anger*	*Rage*
Dissonant (2.7)	Dissonant (1.9)	Dissonant (1.8)
Unsociable (2.7)	Unsociable (2.7)	Unsociable (2.3)
Painful (2.9)	Painful (3.0)	Painful (2.3)
Active (5.0)	Active (5.8)	Active (6.4)
	Bad (2.7)	Bad (2.3)
	High (5.4)	————
	Strong (5.4)	Strong (5.7)
	Masculine (5.2)	————
	Changeable (2.3)	Changeable (2.4)
	Sharp (5.7)	Sharp (5.1)
	Pungent (6.0)	Pungent (5.3)
	Erratic (2.3)	Erratic (2.6)
	Hard (5.5)	Hard (5.2)
	Free (2.9)	————
	Hot (5.7)	Hot (5.5)

DESTRUCTION DIMENSION

Anger	*Rage*
Angular (5.3)	—————————
Excitable (6.4)	Excitable (6.4)
Excited (6.2)	Excited (6.1)
Fast (5.4)	Fast (5.3)
	Heavy (5.2)
	Awkward (2.4)

EXPLORATION DIMENSION

Vigilance	*Expectancy*	*Hopefulness*
Good (5.0)	High (5.0)	Good (5.8)
Strong (5.2)	Interesting (5.0)	Harmonious (5.4)
Constrained (5.3)	Healthy (5.1)	Healthy (5.9)
Active (5.0)	Pleasurable (5.1)	Pleasurable (6.0)
	Excited (5.2)	Excited (5.1)
	Fast (5.1)	High (5.6)
		Strong (5.2)
		Sociable (5.5)

REJECTION DIMENSION

Disgust	*Loathing*
Bad (2.5)	Bad (2.2)
Dissonant (2.4)	Dissonant (2.4)
Pungent (5.0)	Pungent (5.4)
Unsociable (2.9)	Unsociable (2.3)
Painful (2.8)	Painful (2.4)
Constricted (2.8)	—————————
	Strong (5.1)
	Awkward (2.9)
	Heavy (5.1)
	Active (5.1)

DEPRIVATION DIMENSION

Pensiveness	*Sadness*	*Grief*
Low (2.8)	Low (2.2)	Low (2.9)
Private (2.7)	Private (2.3)	—————————
Calm (3.0)	—————————	—————————
Passive (2.5)	—————————	—————————

DEPRIVATION DIMENSION

Pensiveness	*Sadness*	*Grief*
Slow (2.9)	Slow (2.5)	Slow (2.9)
	Bad (2.7)	Bad (2.6)
	Dissonant (2.9)	Dissonant (3.0)
	Unsociable (2.8)	
	Painful (2.0)	Painful (1.8)
	Constrained (6.9)	
	Heavy (5.1)	Heavy (5.3)
	Depressed (1.7)	Depressed (2.4)

With occasional exceptions, the results for all the dimensions are similar to those obtained for the protection dimension; that is, with an increase in the intensity of the emotions, there is an increase in the extremism of judgments and an increase in the number of adjective-pairs to which extreme judgments are made.

Another point worth noting is that these data provide a rough, qualitative index of similarity of emotions. It is possible, for example, to find the number of common adjective-pairs and use these as a rough index. This, of course, would have to be done with emotion words selected at comparable intensity levels.

In the data presented above, hopefulness and joy share eight adjective scales, surprise and joy share five scales, and acceptance and joy share six scales. In each of these cases, the number of scales shared represents almost the total number of scales which have been applied; hopefulness has a total of eight scales, all of which are shared with joy, surprise has seven scales, five of which are shared with joy, and so on. These three positive emotions have very little in common with the other emotions. On the other hand, disgust shares four of its six scales with fear, and sadness shares four of its ten scales with fear.

It is interesting to note that anger has very little in common with most of the other emotions. Of 13 adjective scales which apply to anger, only one of these is common to fear, only one is common to disgust, and none are shared with sadness. This suggests that anger has very different properties from those of fear, disgust and sadness and partially justifies placing anger opposite fear in the present theory. Also consistent with the theory is the finding that anger has more in common with joy than with the three negative emotions just cited: anger shares three of its scales with joy.

The application of the semantic differential to the study of emotion is still in its early development, but even these tentative findings suggest that it is a fruitful tool for exploring the connotative characteristics of emotion terms present in our languages. It might be interesting to apply the technique to people of different ages from childhood on, and to different cultural groups. Among other things, this would contribute to an understanding of the influence of learning on emotional expression.

Experiment 8. The Dimensionality of Emotions

There have been various attempts in the past to try to account for all emotions in terms of simpler and more general dimensions than even the primary emotions provide. The most consistently discussed underlying dimension for all emotions is that of pleasure-pain. This has been discussed by many philosophers since Plato and Epicurus, and many have noted that pleasantness and unpleasantness are the two elementary feelings underlying all emotions.

As Hartmann (1956) summarized this historical trend:

The idea that pleasure and unpleasure are dominant forces in motivating human behavior had, of course, not escaped the attention of earlier thinkers; it goes far back in the history of philosophy and has been strongly emphasized especially by a school of British philosophers. Bentham, to quote one of them, said that nature has put man under the control of two sovereign masters, pain and pleasure.

The first major break with this tradition occurred in 1896, when Wundt postulated *three* underlying dimensions of feeling which he called pleasantness-unpleasant-ness, excitement-quiet, and tension-relaxation. In the next two decades, various attempts were made to identify these dimensions through the use of introspections. In more recent years, the underlying dimensions have sometimes been assumed and sometimes interpreted from the results of factor-analytic studies.

Schlosberg (1954), for example, postulated three dimensions of emotion in connection with his studies of facial expressions, which he calls "pleasantness-unpleasantness, attention-rejection, and level of arousal or intensity." The latter has also been called a dimension of "sleep-tension."

Duffy (1941) argued that all emotions may be thought of in terms of the dimensions of "approach-withdrawal" and high or low activity.

Based on a factor analysis of personality test responses, Jenkins (1955) has proposed two "superfactors," which he identifies with cholinergic (C-factor) and adrenergic (A-factor) activity of the autonomic nervous system, as underlying many personality traits and emotions. Such emotions as anger, buoyancy, and love are represented under the C-factor, while depression, guilt, fear, and lethargy are reflective of the A-factor.

In a review of the literature dealing with conceptual models used to evaluate personality interactions between parent and child, Schaefer (1961) described several factor-analytic studies which have developed two-dimensional schemes. Stagner (1948), for example, proposed the dimensions of "excitement-depression" and "pleasantness-unpleasantness." Kassenbaum, Couch, and Slater (1959) proposed the dimensions of "extroversion-introversion" and "ego-strength ego-weakness." Data from Richards and Simons (1941) are interpreted in terms of the dimensions of "aggressiveness-social apprehensiveness" and "kindness-hostility." Schaefer proposed a model for social and emotional behavior in which the primary dimensions are called "extroversion-introversion" and "hostility-love."

In the experiment by Block (1957) already described,

dealing with the semantic differential, he inferred two major dimensions underlying all the emotions studied, factors which he called "pleasantness-unpleasantness" and "level of activation."

As one examines these various hypotheses about the dimensions underlying emotions, it becomes evident that a pleasure-pain factor appears in all the different approaches (although sometimes under a different terminology, such as love-hostility) and an *intensity* factor as well. Another dimension sometimes used or implied is a kind of expressiveness factor, which some investigators have called extroversion-introversion and others, approach-withdrawal or aggressiveness-apprehensiveness, etc.

In the light of this history, it seemed worthwhile to consider the dimensionality of emotions using a somewhat different approach. The basic question was, if a particular dimension is assumed to be basic, where will the various other emotions and personality traits be judged to fall on this dimension?

Method. Five scales of the semantic differential study which related most closely to the various dimensions proposed in the past were selected. These scales were good-bad, pleasure-pain, excited-depressed, active-passive, and excitable-calm. Figures were plotted showing the distribution of emotions on various pairs of these scales. This is illustrated in Figure 4, where the dimensions of good-bad and active-passive are compared. These scales correlate +0.11 and are, therefore, essentially independent.

The correlations between all five scales are given in Table 6. From inspection of the table, it is evident that our evaluations of good and bad are very closely tied up with our feelings of pleasure and pain, the correlation being +0.91. These two scales do not correlate highly with any of the other scales. On the other hand, the scales excited-depressed, active-passive, and excitable-calm intercorrelate very highly and positively, thus suggesting that there are two basic underlying dimensions in this sample of five scales. One might be called the pleasure-pain di-

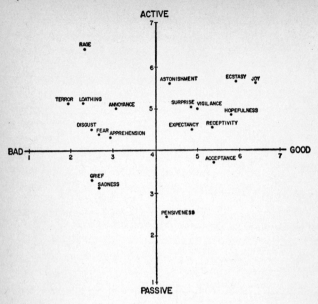

Fig. 4   SEMANTIC DIFFERENTIAL ANALYSIS OF EMOTION WORDS

TABLE 6

Rank-order intercorrelations for five scales
of the semantic differential. N = 19

	Pleasure-Pain	Excited-Depressed	Active-Passive	Excitable-Calm
Good-Bad	+0.91	+0.28	+0.11	−0.22
Pleasure-Pain		+0.39	+0.30	−0.21
Excited-Depressed			+0.89	+0.75
Active-Passive				+0.68

mension and the other an active-passive dimension. Since this study was limited in the number of scales sampled, one can only conclude that *at least* two dimensions are necessary for the specification of the emotions. It is evident that a good deal more research needs to be done on this particular problem.

In the last two chapters, eight experiments which grew out of the theory have been described. These studies range from an analysis of facial expressions to an examination of the connotations of the language of emotions. In each case, it is evident that further research could be done. Thus the theory of emotions presented in this book has value not only in organizing known facts and relating diverse observations, but in suggesting new experiments as well. (It has even been used to study "emotional climate in small groups" [Kronovet, 1960].) Thus it can play an organizing role in the gathering of new data.

10

Implications and New Directions

The view is often defended that sciences should be built up on clear and sharply defined basal concepts. In actual fact no science, not even the most exact, begins with such definitions. The true beginning of scientific activity consists rather in describing phenomena and then in proceeding to group, classify and correlate them. . . . It is only after more searching investigation of the field in question that we are able to formulate with increased clarity the scientific concepts underlying it, and progressively so to modify these concepts that they become widely applicable and at the same time consistent logically. Then indeed, it may be time to immure them in definitions.

—SIGMUND FREUD

The preceding chapters have introduced a theory which conceives of human emotions as deriving from prototypic patterns of reaction identifiable at all evolutionary levels. These basic patterns are limited in number but may fuse, mix, and interact in many different ways and thus produce the great variety of emotions actually observed in nature.

In this chapter an attempt will be made to present some implications of the theory and to show its integrative value. At the same time a tentative answer to most of the questions listed in Chapter 1 will be given.

What Is an Emotion?

In the light of the theory, *an emotion may be defined as a patterned bodily reaction of either destruction, reproduction, incorporation, orientation, protection, deprivation, rejection, or exploration, or some combination of these, which is brought about by a stimulus.*

Emotions are typically transient, adaptive, biological reactions which are usually (but not necessarily) triggered by external stimuli. Both physiological and overt expressive activity are associated with each pattern of reaction; these are the bases for the discriminations usually made in distinguishing different emotions. In man, there may or may not also be introspectively reportable feelings associated with the different emotions. These reactions are organized in some kinds of patterns which differ from one emotion to another (see Chapter 4), or from one emotion-mixture to another. What the pattern is, in any given case, is an empirical question and can only be determined experimentally by a series of successive approximations.

The difficulty of separating emotions clearly from other total body reactions due to drugs, exercise, or fatigue is a complicated problem. Many authors, including Freud, have noted the close interrelations between the effects of illness, fatigue, menstruation, change of life, and emotions, implying that the patterns overlap, mix, and modify one another.

The definition of emotion formulated in this book, although new in form, does have some similarity to views presented by a number of other writers. For example, Wenger (1950) quotes Dunlap, writing in 1916, that "we must follow Lange, rather than James, in making the emotion, not a *result* of the bodily state, but the bodily state itself." Babkin (1950) suggests that emotional behavior is based on an unconditioned reflex and is shown by widespread nervous reactions which involve many organs. Cannon (1929) describes rage, at least, as a "complex attitude which we do not have to learn. . . . It is a constant and uniform type of behavior, having features common in widely scattered races of men and even in lower animals . . . [It has] the characteristics of a simple reflex, such as sneezing or coughing." Fenichel (1946) implies a similar view when he writes: "Affects are originally archaic discharge syndromes that supplant voluntary actions under certain exciting conditions." Arnold Gesell (1950) similarly describes emotions as "patterned phenomena inseparably bound up with patterns of tension, action, and organic attitude." The definition of emotion presented here is a systematic elaboration of views of some other observers.

The Problem of Mixed Emotions

Chapter 8 showed that persisting mixtures of emotions lead to personality traits and that it is possible to analyze the emotional components in each trait. There are, however, other interesting implications of the concept of mixed emotions. For example, if we continue using the analogy of color mixture, we may infer that the mixture of two or more emotions reduces the purity of either one, just as the mixing of two or more colors tends to desaturate them. Some preliminary data suggest that the judged intensity of a mixed emotion is equal to the arithmetic mean of the judged intensity of each of its components. This point needs to be followed up.

Again by analogy, research designed to determine the properties of the primary emotions should attempt to elicit them at high intensity. At lower intensities, the emotions are more likely to be mixed, and the distinctive qualities less evident.

Repression and Control of Emotions

Darwin described the mechanism of repression in some detail in *The Expression of the Emotions in Man and Animals*.

The checking of one habitual movement sometimes requires other slight movements; these latter serving as a means of expression. . . . When tears are restrained with difficulty, as in reading a pathetic story, it is almost impossible to prevent the various muscles . . . from slightly twitching or trembling. . . . With the civilized nations of Europe there is also much difference in the frequency of weeping. Englishmen rarely cry, except under the pressure of the acutest grief; whereas in some parts of the Continent the men shed tears much more readily and freely. . . . Children, when they attempted to prevent a crying-fit or to stop crying would check the contraction of [certain muscles of the forehead]. . . . Laughter is suppressed by the firm contraction of the orbicular muscles of the mouth, which prevents the great zygomatic and other muscles from drawing the lips backwards and upwards. The lower lip is also sometimes held by the teeth. . . . Most of our emotions are so closely connected with their expression, that they hardly exist if the body remains passive. . . . Whatever amount of truth the so-called science of physiognomy may contain, appears to depend . . . on different persons bringing into frequent use different facial muscles, according to their dispositions; the development of these muscles being perhaps thus increased, and the lines or furrows on the face, due to their habitual contraction, being thus rendered deeper and more conspicuous. *The free expression by outward signs of an emotion intensifies it. On the other hand, the repression, as far as this is possible, of all outward signs, softens our emotions* [italics added]. He who gives way to violent gestures will increase his rage; he who does not control the signs of fear will experience fear in a greater degree; and he who remains passive when overwhelmed with grief loses his best chance of recovering elasticity of mind. These results follow partly from the intimate relation which exists between almost all the emotions and their outward manifestations; and partly from the direct influence of exertion on the heart, and consequently on the brain. Even the simulation of an emotion tends to arouse it in our minds.

Darwin thus suggests that repression of emotion may occur through voluntary inhibition of the outward signs of expression of the emotion. Another way of saying this is that we tend to pit one bodily attitude against another or one muscular pattern against another in order to modify or reduce emotional feeling. *This is, in essence, a technique for the control of emotion.* We can control anger, for example, by mixing fear or expectancy to either dilute the anger (the term is used metaphorically) or to inhibit it partially. In ordinary conversation, we often tell someone to keep a stiff upper lip or keep his chin up to hide or overcome sadness. Someone who has learned to hide all his emotions (except the fact that he needs to hide them) is called a dead pan or a poker face.

This same idea has also been expressed by William James. He wrote, "There is no more valuable precept in moral education than this: . . . if we wish to conquer undesirable emotional tendencies in ourselves, we must assiduously, and in the first instance cold-bloodedly, go through the *outward movements* of those contrary dispositions which we prefer to cultivate." James also notes that it is not possible to entirely inhibit emotional expressions since physiological changes (for example, pallor of the face) will still remain.

Some years later, Freud developed this theme. He pointed out that "repression demands a constant expenditure of energy" (1915) and that "the true aim of repression is to suppress the development of affect" (1925). This may be interpreted as indicating that repression involves the development of muscular tensions due to the pitting of one expressive pattern against another.

This is consistent with Luria's observation (1932) that "the active inhibition of the affective symptoms always produces tension." This idea was elaborated most fully in a paper concerned with the role of muscular tension in maladjustment, where considerable evidence was gathered in order to show that chronic muscular tensions arise because adequate motor responses to conditions of conflict or frustration are impeded or blocked (Plutchik, 1954). These tensions reflect a continuous state of readiness of which an individual may often be unaware. From the point of view of the present theory, it may be said that these tensions reflect the mixing of certain relatively opposite emotions. Emotions which are adjacent on the emotion-circle fuse or mix easily (for example, joy + acceptance equals love), while those further removed or more nearly opposite produce greater conflict (joy + fear equals guilt). This increased conflict is reflected by ambivalence and/or vacillation between the emotional components.

Such conflicts have, of course, been reported by many clinicians and are consistent with the views developed here. Suttie (1952) writes that "Hatred . . . owes all its meaning to a demand for love . . . [and] is always ambivalent." Spitz (1960) points out that in infants, "In the emotional interchanges with the love object *both* the libidinal *and* the aggressive drive find their discharge." Fenichel (1946) notes that "ambition represents the fight against shame," that "character traits are the precipitates of instinctual conflicts," and that "in character attitudes, conflicts between impulses and fears may be relatively frozen." These few samples point to the ubiquity of conflict in the clinical setting.

The observations and concepts described above have definite relevance to the problem of psychotherapy.

The Nature of Psychotherapy

Spinoza once wrote: "Hatred is increased through return of hatred, but may be destroyed by love," and that in general, "an affect cannot be restrained nor removed unless by an opposed and stronger affect." William James' comment, cited earlier, is also appropriate here: that is, that the individual who wishes to eliminate undesirable emotional tendencies should "cold-bloodedly" cultivate the opposite or contrary dispositions. Suttie (1952) put the same idea in the following way: "The 'modus operandi' of [psychoanalytic] treatment [is] overcoming hate with love. . . . Therapy involves a social reconciliation at a primitive level of development."

This view is consistent with contemporary learning theory as developed by Mowrer, who pointed out in 1939 that "old habits are eliminated, not by being stamped out or extracted by the roots, but by the functional superimposition of new, more powerful antagonistic habits."

These views imply that one way of thinking about the function of psychotherapy is in terms of the conflict of emotions within the individual. Since maladjusted individuals suffer from severe conflicts which produce various degrees of blocking of activity (Fenichel, 1946), then clearly one of the purposes of therapy is to help the individual resolve his conflicts. This may conceivably be done in several ways.

The individual should be helped to recognize the different emotions which are in conflict within him. This implies that "repressed anger," for example, must really be a mixed emotion for how else would the anger be repressed. Most likely the anger is repressed because of the presence of fear. Similarly, since feelings of resentment are compounded of (at least) disgust and anger, the patient should be gradually encouraged to face these components in their purer form, i.e., what does he wish to reject and what does he wish to destroy? A patient with a neurotically pessimistic outlook on life should be encouraged to gradually face his own feelings of sorrow and fear. Thus one function of psychotherapy is to encourage the individual to go through a process of mental analysis of his mixed emotions in search of the basic components.

A second way of dealing with the problem of conflict is for the therapist to give support to the side of the conflict which is healthier. Such a technique was described briefly by Wolpe (1952) as one in which the patient is encouraged to replace neurotic fear by anger. In a more detailed exposition of his method, Wolpe (1958) describes how it is possible to inhibit "neurotic anxiety" by antagonistic "assertive responses," "relaxation responses," or "sexual responses." Presumably this might work for the other emotion opposites as well: replace neurotic rejection by acceptance, and sadness with pleasure. The problem, of course, is to find the specific means for carrying this out. Very likely the development of so-called active techniques of psychoanalysis by Ferenczi, Reich, Stekel, and others reflects attempts to reduce conflicts by "acting-out" one or another side of the conflict which each patient suffers. Salter's *Conditioned Reflex Therapy* (1949) reflects this same attempt. In this latter case, the therapist provides various rules presumably designed "to increase excitation," but which, in effect, act to replace "undesirable emotional tendencies" with opposite dispositions. For example, patients (all of whom suffer from various degrees of inhibition of action) are told to practice showing their emotions on their face, and to practice saying their spontaneously felt feelings. They are also told to practice contradiction and attack when they honestly differ with someone. These are clearly attempts to change the balance of forces within the conflict. (There are other implications of this approach for the problem of guilt and delinquency, which will be elaborated shortly.)

In summary then, two possible ways of dealing therapeutically with conflicts are to help provide insight into the components of the conflict, and to change the balance of forces within the conflict. It is very likely that in the course of therapy, some of the mixed emotions break up and separate or mix differently, and that this process follows some orderly pattern. Jackson's comment (1954) that as psychotherapy continues "hostility and presumably other emotions [give] place to ambivalence and then friendliness" suggests such a pattern. This implies that in the course of therapy there is some such sequence as: negative mixed emotions → ambivalence → positive mixed emotions. Research directed at this point might be fruitful.

Mental Health and Emotions

Although an analysis of the general nature of mental health is a problem of considerable scope, it is possible to comment meaningfully on the more limited question of the relationship between mental health and emotions.

Many authors have noted that neuroses and psychoses are characterized by a decrease in affective manifestations and that there is generally a restriction or narrowing of the range of emotional responsiveness (Arieti, 1955). Both Rosenberg (1954) and Harris, et al. (1954) have reported that capacity for emotional feeling is a good prognostic sign in neurosis and emotional flatness a poor one.

In clinical practice, typical patients are consistently anxious, depressed, guilty, or resentful; or, as in the case of many delinquents or psychopaths, aggressive, irritable, scornful, or cynical. At the same time, such individuals rarely, if ever, can openly experience and express any other kinds of emotions. The anxious or depressed person may be unable to express his joy or his anger; the psychopath may be unable to express his anxiety or his sadness at the death of another person. One sign of increasing mental health and adjustment is an increase in the range and flexibility of emotional responsiveness and a decrease in the number of strongly conflicting emotions.

Frieda Fromm-Reichmann felt (1950) that mental health includes "potential freedom from fear, anxiety, greed, envy and jealousy," and a capacity "to form durable relations of intimacy and love." It is worth emphasizing that she thought it was not enough to be "free" of these negative emotions; it is also necessary that the individual be capable of experiencing all emotions under appropriate circumstances. There are some realistic situations where fear and jealousy may be appropriate and where anxiety does act as a danger signal. These emotions are pathological only when they persist and disrupt meaningful life activities. Thus, from the point of view of the present theory, mental health is associated with the capacity to experience and express all emotion dimensions; incorporation, orientation, reproduction, protection, deprivation, rejection, exploration, and destruction when the situation calls them forth.

Since emotions are most often reactions to external stimuli, then any persisting pattern of reaction, such as rejection, may reflect either a persisting noxious stimulus in the environment or a pathological over-reaction to a transient situation (as in persisting melancholia).

Of related interest is the problem of symptom formation in psychosomatic medicine. Previous explanations for the individual's choice of symptom have usually pointed to hereditary factors, constitutional weaknesses, or early fixations, all of which act as predisposing factors. Sometimes the correlations found between body types or personality traits and symptoms are used as an explanation of symptom formation.

Although all of these factors may be relevant, a variable not yet systematically explored is the type of emotional reaction an individual typically makes to a stressor. Lacey, et al. (1953) have reported that most individuals react with one dominant physiological pattern, regardless of the nature of the stress. In a situation where the individual is subjected to a long-term stress, this pattern of reaction will predispose the body for breakdown in the dominant reaction system. Thus a cardiovascular reactor type of person, when subjected to repeated or prolonged stress, is more likely to develop some kind of heart or hypertension condition than, say, a gastrointestinal reactor type.

At the same time, it must be recognized that individuals also vary with regard to their preferred methods for inhibiting emotional expression. These methods of inhibition may be just as specific as the methods of expression and lead to other physiological reaction patterns. In general, it would be reasonable to expect that there is a definite connection between the body systems used to express an emotion and those used to suppress or inhibit it. The issues raised here are obviously important ones for research.

The Emotion of Happiness

Most attempts to describe mental health have approached
it negatively from the point of view of the absence of
something undesirable. This was partly true of Fromm-
Reichmann's definition cited above and is true of many
psychoanalytic definitions which emphasize freedom from
anxiety, or freedom from guilt.

In recent years however, there have been some attempts
to describe the positive aspects of mental health, what it
is, rather than what it is not (Smith, 1959). Based on an
analysis of "self-actualizing" people, Maslow (1950) has
suggested such qualities as self-acceptance, spontaneity,
sense of humor, creativeness, and so on, while Jahoda
(1958) has suggested such characteristics as self-acceptance, unifying outlook on life, autonomy, freedom from
need-distortion, social sensitivity, environmental mastery,
etc. But all these attempts leave out of consideration the
question of happiness. As Henry Murray (1954) says:
"One of the strangest, least interpretable symptoms of our
time is the neglect by psychologists of the problem of happiness, that inner state which Plato, Aristotle, and almost
all succeeding thinkers of the first rank assumed to be "the
highest of all goods achievable by action."

The question of the nature of happiness, so much ignored by contemporary psychologists, was briefly commented upon by McDougall (1921) in an interesting way.
He wrote:

> Happiness arises from the harmonious operation of all
> the sentiments of a well-organized and unified per-
> sonality, one in which the principal sentiments sup-
> port one another in a succession of actions all of
> which tend towards the same or closely allied and
> harmonious ends. Hence the richer, the more highly
> developed, the more completely unified or integrated
> is the personality, the more capable is it of sustained
> happiness in spite of inter-current pains of all sorts.

This statement of the sources of happiness is very similar to the one to be presented here. Since one of the cardinal features of all maladjustment is the existence of strong and persisting conflicts, and since improvement is associated with a decrease in conflict, it seems reasonable to consider this as another criterion of mental health. Each individual has a specific set of values, a group of inconsistencies or conflicts among some of them, and a characteristic way of dealing with his own conflicts. Therapy may be conceptualized as an analysis of internal inconsistencies, and as an attempt to integrate conflicting values, emotions and attitudes. We achieve happiness and health as we increase the consistency, stability, and integration of the various systems in conflict within us. This way of formulating the problem may provide a useful guide for research in this area, for it raises such problems as the following. In what terms shall the conflicts within the personality be most effectively described? Is there a developmental progression in the possibilities of conflict? How can the degree of conflict be measured? What are the various ways conflicts may be resolved or reduced? A theory of conflict capable of answering such questions would represent an important advance.

The Nature of Guilt

Another implication of the theory concerns the significance of "guilt" for an understanding of the problem of delinquency.

Guilt is clearly a mixed emotion, and the various procedures described earlier for determining components of complex emotions suggest that there are two major elements in guilt, the feeling of pleasure and the feeling of fear. Guilt is born of the interaction of pleasure and fear. It is based on forbidden joys.

This view is consistent with many observations. Children may feel guilty about bed-wetting or eating forbidden candy. In one case, the fear may be of loss of love; in the other, of physical punishment; pleasures are implicit in both cases.

Quite often a third element becomes involved, the feeling of expectation or anticipation. In such a case, guilt is a result of anticipated pleasure being fused or mixed with anticipated fear.

It is no accident that the idea of guilt is so closely tied to religious concepts of sin. A man who has obtained forbidden pleasures (e.g., committed adultery) has committed a sin and may suffer from fear of punishment (in this life or after). This fusion of fear and pleasure in connection with sin produces guilt. After all, if there were not strong temptations because of anticipated pleasures, there would be no need for social sanctions or punishments, and hence no guilt. This suggests that one of the many functions of religion is as an additional source of fear for certain pleasurable acts whose expression might lead to social conflict. It is thus clear that guilt acts as a possible internal regulator of behavior.

It is interesting to speculate that there are actually several internal regulators of behavior, each of which results from the fusion of fear with one of the other primary emotions. For example, fear + pleasure produces guilt, fear + acceptance produces submissiveness, fear + surprise produces awe, fear + sadness produces despair, fear + disgust produces shame, fear + expectancy produces anxiety.

Each emotion produced by the mixture of fear with another emotion, acts as an inhibitor of certain types of actions.

Because of the dyadic nature of guilt, that is, its composition of two components, it bears certain relations to other mixed emotions which share one or both of the components. Thus guilt will have something in common with other emotions having fear as an element, such as, for example, despair, submission, shame, and anxiety. At the same time, because of the joy component in guilt, it will be related to such emotions as pride, optimism, and friendliness. It would also be quite possible in individuals with strong tendencies toward guilt reactions to find vacillations between some of the above emotions, for example between anxiety and optimism, submissiveness and pride, or despair and friendliness. Such fluctuations have frequently been reported in individuals suffering the throes of religious conversion or conflict. The degree of vacillation between traits or in the strength of guilt depends largely on the relative strength of the pleasure component as compared to the fear component. When they exist in nearly equal strength, there is a tendency toward immobilization of action.

At the same time, it should be recognized that the conflict between joy and fear is not the only approach-avoidance conflict possible. Such conflicts may also occur between anger and fear and between acceptance and rejection, as well as other paired emotions.

One of the factors that makes for variations in the specific quality of guilt is the nature of the emotional reaction to it. Many times we react emotionally to our own emotions. Thus one person may react to his own feeling of guilt with anger, another with sadness, and a third with disgust. Which of these reactions occurs will depend on many factors, one of them being the source of the fear. If, for example, there is fear of loss of love, then the guilt may be mixed with sadness; if the guilt is perceived as an obstacle to the satisfaction of a very strong need, then the guilt may be mixed with anger or resentment, etc.

This raises the question of how an individual deals with his own guilt feelings or defends against them. There are several theoretical possibilities. 1) The guilt feelings may be repressed, i.e., the individual may be unaware of them, even though the effects—the inhibition of action—cannot be eliminated by this technique. 2) The guilt feelings may become rationalized through projection, i.e., hostile forces in the outside world (e.g., policemen, communists, etc.) may be perceived as the basis for the feelings. 3) An intensification or reduction of one or the other element in the conflict may be produced, thus changing the relative balance of forces. Guilt exists when the pleasure and fear elements exist at nearly equal intensity. If there is much pleasure and little fear, or if there is much fear and little pleasure, there is no guilt. Thus any action which changes the relative intensity of the two major components will act to reduce guilt. 4) The guilt may become mixed with other emotions such as anger, sadness, disgust, expectancy, and so on, thus partially diluting it.

These four possibilities are probably the major ways of dealing with guilt. In the light of the various issues discussed above, the problem of delinquency and its treatment may be considered.

Guilt and the Problem of Delinquency

In the last few years, research has increasingly pointed to the fact that, on the average, delinquent children have somewhat different personality traits than non-delinquent children. Among the differences which have been reported is a relatively weak tendency to react with guilt to their own behavior (Plutchik, 1959). Glover (1957) pointed out:

> The outstanding factor which distinguishes the antisocial and delinquent psychopath from the "private" case, both clinically and etiologically, is the quantity of externally directed aggression, either sexual or social. . . . This is coupled with an apparent callousness towards objects and an apparent indifference to consequences, including the stigma. At first sight there appears to be a fault in, or atrophy of, the processes of guilt formation and a weakness in the processes of reality proving, both of which suggest, in turn, an extreme tenuousness of early object relations.

This may be illustrated by a case of an eleven-year-old boy who had been sent to a Child Guidance Clinic because he had thrown a match on a pile of paper in his classroom and set the floor on fire. Some months after he had started at the clinic, he was talking about this incident with the therapist and was asked how he felt about it. He said,

"Well, it would be different now. This time I would pour gasoline on the floor, light a candle and be miles away when the flame reached the floor and set the building on fire."

These children seem to imply that it was not the delinquent act which was wrong, but are sorry only about the fact that they were caught. They cannot punish themselves, as does the neurotic child. They can only experience the feeling of punishment when it is imposed on them from the outside. It is almost as if the neurotic child had the external authority agents of the world firmly incorporated within him, so that one part of him can blame another. For the delinquent psychopath, the external standards of authority have not yet entered.

The fact that many delinquents and psychopaths experience little or no guilt requires explanation in the light of the theoretical considerations discussed above. In general, it means that either the fear or pleasure aspect of the guilt is missing or minimal, or that they have been so fused with other emotions that the distinctive quality of guilt is absent. It is interesting to note that delinquents quite typically are very concerned with eliminating or repressing any signs of fear and put a very high value on courage (fearlessness). One boy described a game he and his friends played in which they would get on their bicycles with extended poles and race full speed toward each other, each attempting to knock the other off his "steed." At a slightly more advanced age, some teen-agers will race their cars toward each other on an open road in an effort to see who "chickens out" first. One of the worst things this kind of child can be called is "yellow."

These examples suggest that the fear aspect of guilt is minimal or repressed and thus so is the guilt. On the other hand, delinquents are frequently reported to have relatively few sources of pleasure. They are often described as restlessly wandering in search of "kicks" because there is "nothing to do," and they have to work at the problem of having fun. One explanation of why community centers may help reduce delinquency is that they provide youngsters with socially sanctioned sources of pleasure, which in turn increase the possibility of guilt or "superego" development.

Another possible reason for the delinquents' lack of guilt is that they are unusually angry and aggressive because they have suffered so many frustrations. In the Glueck study (1950), a significantly higher proportion of delinquents were characterized by feelings of frustration. This aggression tends to interact with whatever guilt there may be and modify it in the direction of resentment, cynicism or scornfulness. These emotions are observed much more commonly in delinquents than in others.

IMPLICATIONS FOR TREATMENT

The theoretical views advanced above lead to certain implications for therapy. If it is assumed that delinquents have a deficit of guilt as compared to normal individuals, and if guilt is assumed to play a valuable role as a self-directed mediator of social sanctions, then it is obvious that delinquents must acquire the capacity to experience guilt.

This, of course, is contrary to what many clinicians describe as necessary in the treatment of neurotic patients, in whom guilt feelings are often excessive and prolonged. It implies that neurotic behavior and delinquent behavior tend toward opposite poles, at least on this dimension of guilt. Observations reported elsewhere (Plutchik, 1959) suggest that there are a number of other dimensions on which delinquents or psychopaths differ from neurotics: the range of expression of emotions, feelings of empathy, self-control, and types of social contacts.

The idea that delinquent children should be treated differently from neurotic children is not at all new. Several decades ago Eichorn, a psychoanalyst in Vienna, treated delinquents successfully by very unorthodox procedures, which he considered consistent with psychoanalytic theory (1955). An English psychoanalyst has recently suggested that "The aims of treatment of the delinquent and the neurotic may lie in opposite directions" (Jackson, 1954).

The delinquent may increase his capacity to experience guilt in several ways. Both his sources of pleasure and his sources of fear must be increased more or less simultaneously. The most effective way of doing this is to try to help him establish positive affectional ties to a therapist or other person. To the extent that this is accomplished, the delinquent has both pleasure in the personal contact and a fear of loss of love.

It is also possible to increase fear through physical punishment or threat of punishment, but this only decreases guilt feelings, since there is no corresponding increase in pleasure. Thus it is evident why the type of delinquency program which simply increases punishments is very unlikely to have any lasting value.

This discussion of guilt and its relation to delinquency has, of course, touched on only one aspect of a very complex social problem. There is no need to re-emphasize the fact that there are many variables influencing delinquency: social, cultural, and historical, as well as personal. The value of this analysis of guilt is that it provides some testable implications and should thus act as a stimulus to further research.

Emotions and Motivations

A theory of emotion should have relevance not only to the various clinical problems already raised, but should contribute in some ways to an understanding of learning and motivation as well. One issue that has been frequently raised in the literature is the question of the relationship between emotion and motivation.

Leeper (1948) has suggested that both motives and emotions "arouse," "sustain," and "direct" behavior and that they should thus be thought of in the same terms. Skinner too (1938, 1953) has indicated that the distinctions between drive and emotion are very thin and that "any extreme deprivation probably acts as an emotional operation." Both drives and emotions are separate from other states, according to Skinner, in that the operations characterizing them "effect concurrent changes in *groups of reflexes.*"

Although it may thus seem that there are some parallels between drives and emotions, yet the distinctions are so important that they cannot be ignored. One of the clearest statements of the differences was made by Woodworth in 1938:

> Anyone will unhesitatingly classify as emotions: anger, fear, disgust, joy and sorrow; and as states of the organism: hunger, thirst, nausea, fatigue, drowsiness, intoxication. Now that physiology has revealed a peculiar organic state in fear and anger, why do we continue to call them emotions and deny that name to fatigue or drowsiness? It is hard to find a valid distinction, unless it be that *the typical emotion is aroused by external stimuli and is directed toward the environment, whereas a state of the organism, such as hunger or fatigue, originates in intraorganic processes and has no direct relation to the environment* [italics added].

Magda Arnold (1960) elaborated on this idea when she wrote: "Emotions themselves are action tendencies like physiological appetites, but they are not activated by a physiological state, nor do they aim toward a specific naturally determined object. . . . Though there is a physiological state specific for each emotion, this state is induced *after* the object seen or appraised."

Thus there may be some valid basis for distinguishing between emotions and motivations. The characteristics of emotion may be summarized in the following way:

1. Emotions are generally aroused by external stimuli.
2. Emotional expression is typically directed toward the particular stimulus in the environment by which it has been aroused.
3. Emotions may be, but are not necessarily or usually, activated by a physiological state.
4. There are no "natural" objects in the environment (like food or water) toward which emotional expression is directed.

5. An emotional state is induced *after* an object is seen or evaluated, and not before.

6. Many emotional states are quite transient; they may appear and disappear rapidly.

The characteristics of motives may be summarized as follows:

1. Motives are aroused by gradually changing internal states of the organism.

2. The basic condition for the arousal of a motive is the *absence* of something. (Emotions are typically aroused by the *presence* of something.)

3. There are certain objects toward which motives "naturally" tend to direct the organism (e.g., food, water, sex mate).

4. Most motives tend to have a rhythmic character, showing more-or-less regular peaks and troughs of intensity.

Since emotions and motives differ in a number of important ways, why should there be such apparent confusion between them in the psychological literature? Two possible explanations follow.

First, there are differences between primary and secondary motives, just as there are differences between primary and mixed emotions. Secondary or acquired motives often do not show a rhythmic fluctuation of intensity (the miser may be greedy regardless of the amount of money he accumulates), nor do they seem to occur as a direct function of recurrent deprivations. On the other hand, mixed emotions may not be transient, but rather persistent (as personality traits) and thus not seem to be clearly dependent upon external stimuli for their appearance.

Second, internal stimuli may, under certain conditions, arouse emotional reactions. Severe deprivation of food may lead to internal pain and a corresponding reaction of fear. Another individual deprived of sex may experience this as a barrier to the satisfaction of a strong need and react with anger or resentment. Thus internal stimuli may occasionally trigger emotional reactions. The failure to distinguish between primary and secondary motives and emotions in discussions of these issues has probably led to much of the confusion present in the literature.

The Influence of Learning on Emotions

There are occasional comments in the literature to the effect that emotions are learned or at least modified by experience. From the point of view of the present theory, the idea that learning affects emotion is true only in a very special sense.

The capacity of an organism to react to stimuli in its environment with any of the prototypic patterns of emotion is essentially an adaptive characteristic of living systems from the amoeba to man. The specific form of the pattern may vary somewhat from one phylogenetic level to another and from birth to senescence, depending upon the development of motor and locomotor capacities and particular body structures. But the prototype patterns of reaction of incorporation, destruction, rejection, and so on, are themselves not learned and are identifiable at all levels.

The influence of learning and experience is twofold: One, an individual may learn to modify or inhibit some of the external expressive signs of emotion (as described in the section on the mixing of emotions); and two, an individual's experience will affect which of the prototypic patterns is most likely to be dominant in his behavior and which are most likely to fuse and interact. The reinforcement history of an individual may also affect the strength and stability of the mixtures which develop.

Differential reinforcement generally acts to influence particular individual responses, whereas emotions refer to complex patterns of reaction to stimuli. Differential reinforcement may affect the object or stimuli toward which aggression or rejection is shown, but it does not create the destruction or rejection pattern itself. A particular reinforcement history may determine how persistent and how generalized an organism's emotional reactions may be, but it does not produce the reactions, which are

more like operant-level type functions, or like unconditioned responses.

The Special Role of Exploration

In order for instrumental learning to occur, some kind
of operant or "spontaneous" behavior must occur first.
Such spontaneous "doing something" is a basic prototypic
pattern upon which most learning depends. Mowrer
(1939) has said that all behavior is "a form of searching
and exploration," and Razran (1961) has reviewed the
voluminous Russian literature on exploration and orienting behavior. We are beginning to recognize the importance of such patterns in conditioning.

Mowrer (1939) has described fear as the conditioned
form of the pain reaction. From the point of view of the
present theory, this might be put somewhat differently.
Since fear is itself a primary emotion and a prototypic
pattern, it seems more fruitful to think of the mixed emotion of anxiety as the conditioned form of the fear reaction.
This means that the combination of fear plus expectancy
produces anxiety, as has been described in earlier chapters.

Since the combination of fear with expectancy produces
the conditioned form of the fear reaction, then the combination of expectancy with each of the other primary
emotions should produce conditioned forms of each of
them. Thus the combination of anger with expectancy
produces the conditioned form of anger, i.e., aggression;
the combination of expectancy with joy produces the conditioned form of the joy reaction or optimism, and so on.
This way of viewing the problem thus reveals an interesting connection between anxiety and aggression, optimism
and pessimism, fatalism and cynicism, all of which are
conditioned forms of the primary emotions.

Concluding Comments

Most of the questions posed in Chapter 1 for a theory of
emotion have been answered, either briefly or fully, in this
chapter. The remaining ones have been touched on in
various earlier sections.

Although all questions cannot be answered fully at this time, partly because much of the necessary data have not been collected, the outlines of a program are becoming visible. The theory of emotion developed in this book provides a systematic framework within which to examine or re-examine many problems in the field, for example: the phylogenetic development of emotions, the ontogenesis of emotions, the relations between emotions and personality, the nature of emotion-terms in natural languages, the influence of learning on the expression, inhibition, and mixing of emotions, the use of scaling techniques for assessing the dimension of intensity, the nature of psychotherapy in terms of emotional interactions, the genetics of emotion, etc. It is evident that the same small number of basic concepts and postulates of the theory are applicable to this wide variety of problems.

The theory presented in this book has been referred to in earlier publications as the "multifactor-analytic theory of emotion," partly because it assumes the existence of a number of basic factors as elements for the analysis of all emotional processes, and partly because it uses an analytic approach (i.e., a breaking down into units). However, it now seems that some other concepts are perhaps equally important and might be stressed: for example, the concept of emotion as deriving from prototypic patterns. Perhaps, therefore, the title of the theory should also partake of evolution as the theory itself develops.

In retrospect, it may be fairly stated that the theory presented here has tried to follow the pattern suggested in Chapter 1. It has tried to comment meaningfully on all the questions raised there; it has attempted to integrate many scattered observations within a single framework; it has predicted some new possibilities; it has shown relationships between apparently diverse areas; and it has acted as a stimulator of research. The theory remains an evolving conception, subject to new data and insights.

Appendix

Some Definitions of Emotion

"My theory . . . is that the bodily changes follow directly the perception of the exciting fact, and that our feeling of the same changes as they occur *is* the emotion."

William James, 1884

"The emotional excitation of specific quality that is the affective aspect of the operation of any one of the principal instincts may be called a primary emotion."

William McDougall, 1921

"An emotion is an hereditary 'pattern-reaction' involving profound changes of the bodily mechanism as a whole, but particularly of the visceral and glandular systems."

John B. Watson, 1924

"All emotions begin from a stimulus which disturbs the balance of the organism. The response varies with the nature of the organism and is more or less complex according to the level of development."

George S. Brett, 1928

"An emotion may thus be provisionally defined as a somatic readjustment which is instinctively aroused by a stimulating situation and which in turn promotes a more effective adaptive response to that situation."

Harvey A. Carr, 1928

"Emotion may be defined as a quality of excitement which accompanies the operation of an instinct, or a kind of drive under which the organism whips itself into action, or a certain kind of response to a certain kind of stimulus."

Madison Bentley, 1928

"For the theory that emotional experiences arise from changes in effector organs is substituted the idea that they are produced by unusual and powerful influences emerging from the region of the thalamus and affecting various systems of cortical neurones."

Walter B. Cannon, 1928

"The peculiar quality of the emotion is added to simple sensation when the thalamic processes are roused."

Walter B. Cannon, 1929

"Emotion is not primarily a kind of response at all but rather a state of strength comparable in many respects with a drive . . ."

Burrhus F. Skinner, 1938

". . . An acute disturbance of the individual as a whole, psychological in origin, involving behavior, conscious experience, and visceral functioning."

Paul T. Young, 1943

"Affects are originally archaic discharge syndromes that supplant voluntary actions under certain exciting conditions."

Otto Fenichel, 1946

"Basically, emotion is an expressive plasmatic motion. . . . These two basic directions of biophysical plasma current [from the center toward the periphery, or vice versa] correspond to the two basic affects of the psychic apparatus, pleasure and anxiety."

Wilhelm Reich, 1949

"Emotion [means] the same thing as (1) an introspectively given affective state, usually mediated by acts of interpretation; (2) the whole set of internal physiological changes, which help (ideally) the return to normal equilibrium between the organism and its environment, and (3) the various patterns of overt behavior, stimulated by the environment and implying constant interactions with it, which are expressive of the stirred-up physiological state (2) and also the more or less agitated psychological state (1)."

John R. Reid and Stanley Cobb, 1950

"Feeling, in the sense of affect, arises from involuntary motor attitude, maintained as readiness or wish, and held in leash pending the lifting of whatever form of interfering mechanism, or functional barrier, is holding up the action."

Nina Bull, 1951

"The common idioms 'in love,' 'in fear,' 'in anger,' suggest a definition of an emotion as a conceptual state, in which the special response is a function of circumstances in the history of the individual."

Burrhus F. Skinner, 1953

"We define an emotion . . . as a particular state of strength or weakness in one or more responses induced by any one of a class of operations. We may make as many distinctions as we wish between separate emotions . . ."

Burrhus F. Skinner, 1953

"Emotion is activity and reactivity of the tissues and organs innervated by the autonomic nervous system. It may involve, but does not necessarily involve, skeletal muscular response or mental activity."

Marion A. Wenger, 1956

"Emotion can be both organizing (making adaptation to the environment more effective) and disorganizing, both energizing and debilitating, both sought after and avoided."

Donald O. Hebb, 1958

"We define 'emotion' broadly as: 1) episodes or sequences of overt and incipient somatic adjustment, 2) often loosely patterned and variable, 3) usually with concurrent exciting sensory effects, perhaps also perceptual attitudes characterizable as desirable or undesirable, pleasant or unpleasant, 4) related to the intensity effects or perceptual meaning of a stimulus, 5) synergic with organic changes of A- (approach) or W- (withdrawal) types."

Theodore C. Schneirla, 1959

". . . the felt tendency toward anything intuitively appraised as good (beneficial), or away from anything intuitively appraised as bad (harmful). This attraction or aversion is accompanied by a pattern of physiological changes organized toward approach or withdrawal. The patterns differ for different emotions."

Magda Arnold, 1960

"An emotion may be defined as a patterned bodily reaction of either destruction, reproduction, incorporation, orientation, protection, deprivation, rejection or exploration, or some combination of these, which is brought about by a stimulus."

Robert Plutchik, 1962

References

ALMY, T. P. Experimental studies on the irritable colon. *Amer. J. Med.* 1951, *10*, 60-67.

ANDERSON, E. E. The interrelationship of drives in the male albino rat. *Comp. Psychol. Monogr.* 1938, *14*, No. 6.

ARIETI, S. *Interpretation of schizophrenia.* New York: Brunner, 1955.

ARNOLD, MAGDA B. Physiological differentiation of emotional states. *Psychol. Rev.* 1945, *52*, 35-48.

ARNOLD, MAGDA B. *Emotion and personality.* New York: Columbia Univ., 1960. 2 vols.

AX, A. F. The physiological differentiation of fear and anger in humans. *Psychosom. Med.* 1953, *15*, 433-442.

BABKIN, B. P. The conditioning of emotions. In M. L. Reymert (Ed.), *Feelings and emotions.* New York: McGraw-Hill, 1950. Ch. 3.

BANHAM, K. M. The development of affectionate behavior in infancy. *Pedagog. Semin. and J. genet. Psychol.* 1950, *76*, 283-289.

BEKHTEREV, V. M. Emotions as somatomimetic reflexes. In M. L. Reymert (Ed.), *Feelings and emotions:* The Wittenberg Symposium. Worcester, Mass.: Clark Univ., 1928.

BERKOWITZ, L. The expression and reduction of hostility. *Psychol. Bull.* 1958, *55*, 257-283.

BERLYNE, D. E. *Conflict, arousal, and curiosity.* New York: McGraw-Hill, 1960.

BINDRA, D. Organization in emotional and motivated behavior. *Canad. J. Psychol.* 1955, *9*, 161-167.

BLOCK, J. Studies in the phenomenology of emotions. *J. abnorm. soc. Psychol.* 1957, *54*, 358-363.

BOTT, H. M. Personality development in young children. *Child Devel. Series, No. 2.* Toronto: Univ. Toronto, 1934.

BOWLBY, J. Grief and mourning in infancy and early childhood. In *Psychoanalytic study of the child.* New York: International Univ., 1960. Vol. 15.

BRIDGER, A. W. and REISER, M. F. A preliminary report of psychophysiological studies of the neonate. *Psychosom. Med.* 1959, *21*, 265-276.

BROWN, J. S. and FARBER, I. E. Emotions conceptualized as intervening variables with suggestions toward a theory of frustration. *Psychol. Bull.* 1951, *48*, 465-495.

BULL, NINA. Towards a clarification of the concept of emotion. *Psychosom. Med.* 1945, *7*, 210-214.

BULL, NINA. The attitude theory of emotion. New York: *Nerv. & Ment. Dis., Monog.* No. 81, 1951.

BULL, NINA. The attitude theory of emotion. *Internat. Rec. Med.* 1952, *165*, 216-220.

BULL, NINA and GIDRO-FRANK, L. Emotions induced and studied in hypnotic subjects II. *J. Nerv. Ment. Dis.* 1950, *112*, 97-120.

BURN, J. H. Relation of adrenaline to acetylcholine in the nervous system. *Physiol. Rev.* 1945, *25*, 377-394.

BURT, C. The factorial study of emotions. In M. L. Reymert (Ed.), *Feelings and emotions.* New York: McGraw-Hill, 1950. Ch. 46.

BUZBY, D. E. The interpretation of facial expressions of emotion. *Amer. J. Psychol.* 1924, *35*, 602-604.

CANNON, W. B. The James-Lange theory of emotion. *Amer. J. Psychol.* 1927, *39*, 106-124.

CANNON, W. B. Neural organization for emotional expression. In M. L. Reymert (Ed.), *Feelings and emotions:* The Wittenberg Symposium. Worcester, Mass.: Clark Univ., 1928.

CANNON, W. B. *Bodily changes in pain, hunger, fear and rage.* New York: Appleton, 1929.

CANNON, W. B. *The wisdom of the body.* New York: Norton, 1939.

CARR, H. A. *Psychology, a study of mental activity.* New York: Longmans, Green, 1929.

CATTELL, R. B. *Description and measurement of personality.* Yonkers, N. Y.: World Book, 1946.

CHRISTY, R. *Proverbs, maxims and phrases of all ages.* New York: Putnam's, 1887.

CLAPARÈDE, E. Feelings and emotions. In M. L. Reymert (Ed.), *Feelings and emotions:* The Wittenberg Symposium. Worcester, Mass.: Clark Univ., 1928.

CONANT, J. B. *On understanding science.* New Haven: Yale Univ., 1947.

DARWIN, C. *The expression of the emotions in man and animals.* New York: Appleton-Century, 1920.

DAVIS, R. C. The specificity of facial expressions. *J. Gen. Psychol.* 1934, *10*, 42-58.

DAVIS, R. C., BUCHWALD, A. M. and FRANKMAN, R. W. Autonomic and muscular responses, and their relation to simple stimuli. *Psychol. Monog.* 1955, 69. Whole No. 405.

DAVIS, S. W. Stress in combat. *Sci. Amer.* 1956, *194*, 31-35.

DIETHELM, O., FLEETWOOD, M. F. and MILHORAT, ADE T. The predictable association of certain emotions and biochemical changes in the blood. In H. G. Wolff (Ed.), *Life stress and bodily disease.* Baltimore: Williams and Wilkins, 1950.

DUFFY, ELIZABETH. The conceptual categories of psychology; a suggestion for revision. *Psychol. Rev.* 1941, *48*, 177-203.

DUFFY, ELIZABETH. The concept of energy mobilization. *Psychol. Rev.* 1951, *58*, 30-40.

DUFFY, ELIZABETH. The psychological significance of the concept of "arousal" or "activation." *Psychol. Rev.* 1957, *64*, 265-275.

DUNBAR, F. *Emotions and bodily changes.* New York: Columbia Univ., 1947.

DYKMAN, R. A., REESE, W. G., GALBRECHT, C. R. and THOMASSON, PEGGY J. Psychophysiological reactions to novel stimuli: measurements, adaptation, and relationship of psychological and physiological variables in the normal human. *Annals New York Acad. Sci.* 1959, *79*, 43-107.

EICHORN, A. *Wayward youth.* New York: Meridian, 1955.

EINSTEIN, A. and INFELD, L. *The evolution of physics.* New York: Simon and Schuster, 1938.

FARBER, I. E. and WEST, L. J. Conceptual problems of research on emotions. *Psychiat. Res. Repts. 12. Amer. Psychiat. Assoc.* 1960.

FENICHEL, O. *The psychoanalytic theory of neurosis.* London: Routledge and Kegan Paul, 1946.

FRANKLE, A. H. Psychometric investigation of the relationship between emotional repression and the occurrence of psychosomatic symptoms. *Psychosom. Med.* 1952, *14*, 252-255.

FREEMAN, E. *Principles of general psychology.* New York: Holt, 1939.

FREUD, ANNA. Discussion of Dr. John Bowlby's paper. In *Psychoanalytic study of the child.* New York: International Univ., 1960. Vol. 15.

FREUD, ANNA and BURLINGHAM, D. T. *Infants without families; the case for and against residential nurseries*. New York: International Univ., 1944.

FREUD, S. *Beyond the pleasure principle*. London: Hogarth, 1922.

FREUD, S. The unconscious. (1915) In *Collected papers*. London: Hogarth, 1925. Vol. 4.

FREUD, S. Formulations regarding the two principles in mental functioning. In *Collected papers*. London: Hogarth, 1925. Vol. 4.

FREUD, S. *An autobiographical study*. New York: Norton, 1935.

FREUD, S. *The problem of anxiety*. New York: Norton, 1936.

FREUD, S. *A general introduction to psychoanalysis*. New York: Permabooks, 1953.

FROIS-WITTMAN, J. Judgement of facial expressions. *J. exp. Psychol.* 1930, 7, 325-341.

FROMM-REICHMAN, FRIEDA. *Principles of intensive psychotherapy*. Chicago: Univ. Chicago, 1950.

FUNKENSTEIN, D. H. The physiology of fear and anger. *Sci. Amer.* 1955, 192, 74-80.

FUNKENSTEIN, D. H., KING, S. H. and DROLETTE, M. E. *Mastery of stress*. Cambridge: Harvard Univ., 1957.

GELLHORN, E. Recent contributions to the physiology of emotions. *Psychiatric Res. Rep.* 1960, 12, 209-223.

GESELL, A. Emotion from the standpoint of developmental morphology. In M. L. Reymert (Ed.), *Feelings and emotions*. New York: McGraw-Hill, 1950. Ch. 32.

GLOVER, E. Observations on treating psychopathic delinquents. *J. Assoc. Psychiat. Treat. Offenders.* 1957, 1, 1-3.

GLUECK, S. and GLUECK, ELEANOR. *Unraveling juvenile delinquency*. New York: Commonwealth Fund, 1950.

GOLIGHTLY, C. L. The James-Lange theory: a logical postmortem. *Phil. of Sci.* 1953, 20, 286-299.

GOODENOUGH, FLORENCE L. *Anger in young children*. Minn.: Univ. Minn., 1931.

GRACE, W. J., WOLF, S. and WOLFF, H. *The human colon*. New York: Hoeber, 1951.

GREENACRE, PHYLLIS. Experiences of awe in childhood. In *The psychoanalytic study of the child*. New York: International Univ., 1956. Vol. II.

GUILFORD, J. P. and ZIMMERMAN, W. S. Fourteen dimensions of temperament. *Psychol. Monog.* 1956, 70, No. 10. Whole No. 417.

GUTTMAN, L. A new approach to factor analysis: The Radex. In P. F. Lazarsfeld (Ed.), *Mathematical thinking in the social sciences*. Glencoe, Ill.: Free Press, 1954.

HANAWALT, N. G. The role of the upper and lower parts of the face as a basis for judging facial expression. *J. gen. Psychol.* 1944, *31*, 23-36.

HARLOW, H. F. Affectional responses in the infant monkey. *Science.* 1959, *130*, 421-432.

HARLOW, H. F. The nature of love. *Amer. Psychol.* 1958, *13*, 673-685.

HARRIS, A. and NORIS, V. Clinical signs, diagnosis and prognosis in the functional psychoses. *J. ment. Sci.* 1954, *100/420*, 727-731.

HARTMANN, H. Notes on the reality principle. In *The psychoanalytic study of the child*. New York: International Univ., 1956. Vol. II.

HEBB, D. O. Emotion in man and animal: an analysis of the intuitive processes of recognition. *Psychol. Rev.* 1946, *53*, 88-106.

HEBB, D. O. *The organization of behavior*. New York: Wiley, 1949.

HILL, D. C. *The communication of emotions by facial expressions in the light of a new theory*. M.A. Thesis, Hofstra College, Hempstead, New York, 1955.

HUIZINGA, J. *Homo ludens; a study of the play element in culture*. New York: Roy, 1950.

IVERSON, M. A. A factor analysis of anger ratings assigned to five classes of motivational situations. *Psychol. Monog.* 1955, *69*, No. 15. Whole No. 400.

JACKSON, LYDIA. *Aggression and its interpretation*. London: Methuen, 1954.

JAHODA, MARIE. *Current concepts of positive mental health*. New York: Basic, 1958.

JAMES, W. What is emotion? *Mind.* 1884, *19*, 188-205.

JAMES, W. *The principles of psychology*. New York: Holt, 1910.

JENKINS, T. N. The neutral theory of personality: new evidence and a review of the argument. *Trans. N. Y. Acad. Sci.* 1955, *17*, 315-330.

JORGENSEN, C. A theory of the elements in the emotions. In M. L. Reymert (Ed.), *Feelings and emotions:* The Wittenberg Symposium. Worcester, Mass.: Clark Univ., 1928.

KASSENBAUM, G. G., COUCH, A. J. and SLATER, P. E. The factorial dimensions of the MMPI. *J. Consult. Psychol.* 1959, *23*, 226-236.

KEMPF, E. J. Neuroses as conditioned, conflicting, holistic, attitudinal, acquisitive avoidant reactions. *Annals New York Acad. Sci.* 1953, *56*, 307-329.

KEMPF, E. J. Basic biodynamics. *Annals New York Acad. Sci.* 1958, *73*, 869-910.

KINSEY, A. C., POMEROY, W. B. and MARTIN, C. E. *Sexual behavior in the human male.* Philadelphia: Saunders, 1948.

KLINEBERG, O. Emotional expression in Chinese literature. *J. abnorm. soc. Psychol.* 1938, *33*, 517-520.

KROGH, A. *The anatomy and physiology of capillaries.* New Haven: Yale Univ., 1922.

KRONOVET, ESTHER. The development of a multiple-choice technique for assessing emotional climate in small discussion groups. Paper presented at the 16th International Congress of Psychology. Bonn, Germany, 1960.

LACEY, J. I., BATEMAN, D. E. and VAN LEHN, R. Autonomic response specificity: An experimental study. *Psychosom. Med.* 1953, *15*, 8-21.

LACEY, J. I. and SMITH, R. L. Conditioning and generalization of unconscious anxiety. *Science.* 1954, *120*, 1045-1052.

LANDAUER, K. Affects, passions and temperament. *Internat. J. Psychoanal.* 1938, *19*, 388-415.

LANDIS, C. Studies of emotional reactions II. General behavior and facial expression. *J. Comp. Psychol.* 1924, *4*, 447-509.

LEEPER, R. W. A motivational theory of emotion to replace "emotion as disorganized response." *Psychol. Rev.* 1948, *55*, 5-21.

LIDDELL, H. The role of vigilance in the development of animal neurosis. In P. Hoch and J. Zubin (Eds.), *Anxiety.* New York: Grune and Stratton, 1950.

LINDSLEY, D. B. Emotion. In S. S. Stevens (Ed.), *Handbook of experimental psychology.* New York: Wiley, 1951. Ch. 14.

LOOMIS, A. M. A technique for observing the social behavior of nursery school children. *Child Devel. Monog.* New York: Teachers College, Columbia Univ., 1931. No. 5.

LURIA, A. R. *The nature of human conflicts.* New York: Liveright, 1932.

MAHL, G. F. The relationship between acute and chronic fear and the gastric acidity and blood sugar levels in Macaca rhesus monkeys. *Psychosom. Med.* 1952, *14*, 182-210.

MAHL, G. F. Physiological changes during chronic fear. *Annals New York Acad. Sci.* 1953, *56*, 240-252.

MALMO, R. B. Anxiety and behavioral arousal. *Psychol. Rev.* 1957, *64*, 276-287.

MALMO, R. B. Activation: A neuropsychological dimension. *Psychol. Rev.* 1959, *66*, 367-386.

MASLOW, A. H. Self-actualizing people: A study of psychological health. *Personality Symposia.* 1950. No. 1.

MASSERMAN, J. H. A biodynamic psychoanalytic approach to the problems of feeling and emotion. In M. L. Reymert (Ed.), *Feelings and emotions.* New York: McGraw-Hill, 1950. Ch. 4.

McDOUGALL, W. *An introduction to social psychology.* Boston: Luce, 1921.

McDOUGALL, W. Emotion and feelings distinguished. In M. L. Reymert (Ed.), *Feelings and emotions:* The Wittenberg Symposium. Worcester, Mass.: Clark Univ., 1928.

MEYERS, R. The nervous system and general semantics. IV. The fiction of the thalamus as the neural center of emotions, etc.: *A Rev. Gen. Semantics.* 1950, *7*, 104-127.

MITTLEMANN, B. and WOLFF, H. G. Emotions and skin temperature: observations on patients during psychotherapeutic (psychoanalytic) interviews. *Psychosom. Med.* 1943, *5*, 211-231.

MOWRER, O. H. Anxiety and learning. *Psychol. Rev.* 1939, *46*, 553-565.

MURPHY, G. and MURPHY, Lois B. *Experimental social psychology.* New York: Harper, 1931.

MURRAY, H. A. Toward a classification of interaction. In T. Parsons and E. A. Shils (Eds.), *Toward a general theory of action.* Cambridge: Harvard Univ., 1954.

NISSEN, H. W. Phylogenetic comparisons. In S. S. Stevens (Ed.), *Handbook of experimental psychology.* New York: Wiley, 1951.

NOWLIS, V. and NOWLIS, HELEN H. The description and analysis of moods. *Annals New York Acad. Sci.* 1956, *65*, 345-355.

OPPENHEIMER, R. Analogy in science. *Amer. Psychol.* 1956, *11*, 127-135.

OSGOOD, C. E., SUCI, G. J. and TANNENBAUM, P. H. *The measurement of meaning.* Urbana: Univ. Ill., 1957.

OSTOW, M. Affects in psychoanalytic theory. Symposium on

"Current Theories of Emotion" at *Amer. Psychol. Assoc.* meeting. Cincinnati, 1959.

PASQUARELLI, B. and BULL, NINA. Experimental investigation of the mind-body continuum in affective states. *J. Nerv. Ment. Dis.* 1951, *113*, 512-521.

PHILLIPS, L. Some problems in the evaluation of pharmacotherapy. In: *Psychopharmacology: problems in evaluation.* Nat. Acad. Sci.—Nat. Res. Coun. Publ. 583, 1956.

PIERON, H. Feelings and emotions. In M. L. Reymert (Ed.), *Feelings and emotions:* The Wittenberg Symposium. Worcester, Mass.: Clark Univ., 1928.

PLUTCHIK, R. Further remarks on the hypothetical construct. *J. Psychol.* 1954, *37*, 59-64.

PLUTCHIK, R. The role of muscular tension in maladjustment. *J. gen. Psychol.* 1954, *50*, 45-62.

PLUTCHIK, R. Some problems for a theory of emotion. *Psychosom. Med.* 1955, *17*, 306-310.

PLUTCHIK, R. Further comments on the definition of emotion. *Psychol. Rec.* 1957, *7*, 123-124.

PLUTCHIK, R. Outlines of a new theory of emotion. *Trans. N. Y. Acad. Sci.* 1958, *20*, 394-403.

PLUTCHIK, R. Comments on the problem of individual differences in psychophysiological research. *Office of Naval Research Symposium Report,* APR-30, 1958.

PLUTCHIK, R. Implications of a neurosis-delinquency continuum. *J. Assoc. Psychiat. Treat. Offenders.* 1959, *3*, 3-4.

RAPAPORT, D. *Emotions and memory.* New York: International Univ., 1950.

RAZRAN, G. The observable unconscious and the inferable conscious in current Soviet psychophysiology: interoceptive conditioning, semantic conditioning, and the orienting reflex. *Psychol. Rev.* 1961, *68*, 81-147.

REICH, W. *The function of the orgasm.* New York: Orgone Institute, 1942. Vol. I.

REICH, W. *Character analysis.* New York: Noonday, 1949. 3rd edition.

REICHSMAN, F. "Ulcer clue found in baby's stomach." Report in *New York Times,* May 6, 1955.

RICHARDS, T. W. and SIMONS, MARJORIE P. The Fels Child Behavior Scales. *Genet. Psychol. Monogr.* 1941, *24*, 259-309.

ROSENBERG, S. The relationship of certain personality factors to prognosis in psychotherapy. *J. Clin. Psychol.* 1954, *10*, 341-345.

SALTER, A. *Conditioned reflex therapy.* New York: Creative Age, 1949.

SAUL, L. J. Hostility in cases of essential hypertension. *Psychosom. Med.* 1939, *1*, 153-161.

SCHAEFER, E. S. Converging conceptual models for maternal behavior and for child behavior. In J. Glidewell (Ed.), *Parental attitudes and child behavior.* Springfield, Ill.: Thomas, 1961.

SCHLOSBERG, H. Three dimensions of emotion. *Psychol. Rev.* 1954, *61*, 81-88.

SCHNEIRLA, T. C. An evolutionary and developmental theory of biphasic processes underlying approach and withdrawal. In M. R. Jones (Ed.), *Nebraska symposium on motivation.* Lincoln: Univ. Nebr., 1959.

SCHUR, M. Discussion of Dr. John Bowlby's paper. In *Psychoanalytic study of the child.* New York: International Univ., 1960. Vol. 15.

SCOTT, J. P. *Animal behavior.* Chicago: Univ. Chicago, 1958.

SEARS, R. R., HOVLAND, C. I. and MILLER, N. B. Minor studies of aggression. *J. Psychol.* 1940, *9*, 215-295.

SELYE, H. *The physiology and pathology of exposure to stress.* Montreal: Acta., 1950.

SKINNER, B. F. *The behavior of organisms.* New York: Appleton-Century-Crofts, 1938.

SKINNER, B. F. *Science and human behavior.* New York: Macmillan, 1953.

SMITH, M. B. Research strategies toward a conception of positive mental health. *Amer. Psychol.* 1959, *14*, 673-681.

SPINOZA, BENEDICT DE. On the origin and nature of the affects. In *Ethics,* Encyclopaedia Britannica Syntopticon. Chicago: 1952.

SPITZ, R. A. *No and yes.* New York: International Univ., 1957.

SPITZ, R. A. Discussion of Dr. Bowlby's paper. In *Psychoanalytic study of the child.* New York: International Univ., 1960. Vol. 15.

SPITZ, R. A. and WOLF, K. M. Anaclitic depression; an inquiry into the genesis of psychiatric conditions in early childhood. In *The psychoanalytic study of the child.* New York: International Univ., 1956. Vol. II.

STAGNER, R. *Psychology of personality.* New York: McGraw-Hill, 1948.

STEVENSON, B. *The home book of proverbs, maxims and familiar phrases.* New York: Macmillan, 1948.

SULLIVAN, H. S. *Clinical studies in psychiatry*. New York: Norton, 1956.

SUTTIE, I. D. *The origins of love and hate*. New York: Julian Press, 1952.

THOMPSON, JANE. Development of facial expressions of emotion in blind and seeing children. *Arch. Psychol*. New York, 1941, No. 264, 1-47.

THORPE, W. H. Some implications of the study of animal behavior. *Sci. Monthly*. 1957, 84, 309-320.

TOLMAN, E. C. A behavioristic account of the emotions. (1923) In *Behavior and psychological man*. Berkeley: Univ. Calif., 1958.

TOLMAN, E. C. A stimulus-expectancy, need-cathexis psychology. In *Behavior and psychological man*. Berkeley: Univ. Calif., 1958.

TURNER, W. J. Some phylogenetic roots of human behavior. *Trans. New York Acad. Sci*. 1957, 20, 192-198.

VALENTINE, W. L. *Experimental foundations of general psychology*. New York: Rinehart, 1941.

WATSON, J. B. *Psychology from the standpoint of a behaviorist*. Phila.: Lippincott, 1924.

WENGER, M. A. Emotion as visceral action: an extension of Lange's theory. In M. L. Reymert (Ed.), *Feelings and emotions*. New York: McGraw-Hill, 1950. Ch. 1.

WILDER, J. The law of initial value in neurology and psychiatry: facts and problems. *J. Nerv. Ment. Dis*. 1957, 175, 73-86.

WOLF, S. and WOLFF, H. G. Evidence on the genesis of peptic ulcer in men. *J. Amer. Med. Assoc*. 1942, 120, 670-675.

WOLFF, H. G. *Life stress and bodily disease*. Baltimore: Williams and Wilkins, 1950.

WOLFF, H. G. Life situations, emotions, and bodily disease. In M. L. Reymert (Ed.), *Feelings and emotions*. New York: McGraw-Hill, 1950. Ch. 24.

WOLPE, J. Objective psychotherapy of the neuroses. *S. Afr. Med. J*. 1952, 26, 825-829.

WOLPE, J. *Psychotherapy by reciprocal inhibition*. Stanford, Stanford Univ., 1958.

WOODWORTH, R. S. How emotions are identified and classified. In M. L. Reymert (Ed.), *Feelings and emotions:* The Wittenberg Symposium, Worcester, Mass.: Clark Univ., 1928.

WOODWORTH, R. S. *Experimental psychology*. New York: Holt, 1938.

YOUNG, P. T. Studies in affective psychology. *Amer. J. Psychol.* 1927, *38*, 157-193.

YOUNG, P. T. *Emotion in man and animals.* New York: Wiley, 1943.

YOUNG, P. T. The role of hedonic processes in the organization of behavior. *Psychol. Rev.* 1952, *57*, 249-262.

YOUNG, P. T. The role of affective processes in learning and motivation. *Psychol. Rev.* 1959, *66*, 104-125.

ZANGWILL, O. L. The theory of emotion: A correspondence between J. I. MacCurdy and Morton Prince. *Brit. J. Psychol.* 1948, *39*, 1-11.

Author Index

Subject Index